Library of
Davidson College

Library of
David

THEATER OF FINE DEVICES

Theater of Fine Devices
Thomas Combe

Introduction by Mary V. Silcox

Scolar Press

The Introduction © copyright Mary V. Silcox, 1990

All rights reserved. No part of this publication may be reproduced, stored in a retrieval system, or transmitted in any form or by any means, electronic, mechanical, photocopying, recording, or otherwise without the prior permission of the publisher.

Published by
SCOLAR PRESS
Gower Publishing Company Limited
Gower House
Croft Road
Aldershot
Hants GU11 3HR
England

Gower Publishing Company
Old Post Road
Brookfield
Vermont 05036
USA

British Library Cataloguing in Publication Data
Combe, Thomas
　Theater of fine devices.
　I. Title
　821'.3

　ISBN 0–85967–769–9

Printed in Great Britain by Galliard (Printers) Ltd.

General Editors' Preface

This new series of Emblem Books from Scolar Press is published to meet the developing interest in this Renaissance form, and to attempt to satisfy the needs of scholars and students, currently engaged in research, who require access to the texts in an edition as close to the original as possible. This series has been created in association with Glasgow University Library which houses one of the largest and most comprehensive collections of Emblem Books in the world and is an important centre for research into the subject. The University Library contains originals of these texts, collected by Sir William Stirling Maxwell (1818–1878) and bequeathed to the University by his son Sir John Stirling Maxwell. Clearly, with such a large collection – there are over 1700 items – selection procedure proved difficult at first, but the general editors decided that the objective initially should be to provide those texts from the late sixteenth and early seventeenth centuries which would be

GENERAL EDITORS' PREFACE

most referred to by the students of the period, or which are too scarce to be easily consulted. Detailed enquiries led to the drawing up of an extensive short list, from which the decision on which texts to produce first was made. We would welcome comments on the selections, suggestions for further volumes, and hope that the introductions will provide the stimulus for further exploration into this fascinating field.

> David Weston: Glasgow University Library
> Charles Moseley: Cambridge University
> Brian Last: Scholar Press

Introduction

Biography of Combe

The starting point for any discussion of Thomas Combe would also appear to be the concluding point of any certain information about him – Francis Meres's reference to him as an emblematist in *Palladis Tamia* (1598): 'As the Latines have these *Emblematists, Andreas Alciatus, Reusnerus*, and *Sambucus*: so we have these, *Geffrey Whitney, Andrew Willet* and *Thomas Combe*' (fol. 285v). This seems to be the only contemporary mention of Thomas Combe the emblematist, and his identity was apparently lost. It now seems likely, however, that the Thomas Combe who translated *The Theater of Fine Devices* is the Thomas Combe whose initials appear on the title-page of 'An Anatomie of the Metamorphosed Ajax' in *A New Discourse of a Stale Subject Called The Metamorphosis of Ajax* (1596), Sir John Harington's witty treatise on his invention of the w.c., or flush toilet. Elizabeth Story Donno convincingly argues in her edition of that work that Harington's personal servant, Thomas Combe, wrote and illustrated the 'Anatomie' section of the three-part *Metamorphosis*, and she suggests that this Thomas Combe is also the translator of *The Theater*.[1]

Although the position of servant would seem at first to preclude literary activity, in this case the reverse is actually true. Harington was not only well read, but himself a poet and translator, and the master-servant relationship was evidently a close one. Combe wrote a number of letters to Harington in Ireland and recommended books to him; Harington in return wrote Combe a long letter describing the conditions during Essex's 1599 expedition.[2] Harington's translation of *Orlando Furioso* (1591) and his *Metamorphosis* (1596) were both published by Nathaniel Field, as was *The Theater* (c.1593).

From the remarks made by and about Combe in the *Metamorphosis* it seems all but certain he is the translator of *The Theater*. These remarks also suggest the possibility that Combe himself copied the woodcuts from *Le Theatre des bons engins* for *The Theater*. Combe's artistic talents are commented upon by both Harington's cousin, Master Edward Sheldon, in his 'Prefatory Letter from Philostilpnos' ('M. Combe . . . can paint pretily,' p. 57) and by Harington, who explains that 'my servant Thomas (whose pensil can performe more in this matter than my pen) will set downe the forme of this [privie] by it selfe in the end hereof' (p. 172).

INTRODUCTION

Combe, however, does not 'set downe' Harington's invention in an unadorned state; he continued Harington's witty, allusive, and learned discourse. On the title page of 'An Anatomie' he describes himself as 'T.C. Traveller, Aprentice in Poetrie, Practiser in Musicke, professor of Painting' (p. 187). Later in the 'Anatomie' he gives some facts about himself to prove his suitability to the task:

> Wherefore by the Priviledge of this Charter [of Painters and Poets] (as also by a Pattent I have of serving two prentiships) I will go somewhat beyond the bare wordes of my commission, and yet not swarve much from the charge that is layd upon me. For Sir, I would you knew it, though I never troubled the schooles at Oxford, with any disputes or degrees, yet I carried there a good schollers bookes after him.[3]

He translates a line from Persius into an English iambic pentameter couplet (p. 192), repeats scholars' jokes (pp. 197 and 201), and quotes from Horace, Cicero, and Sidney's *Astrophel and Stella*. He goes on to compare himself to Harington, saying they are both of an age, similar in complexion and disposition, 'one of my kin did teach him at Eaton, & one of his kin taught me at Oxford,' both have been beyond the sea but not out of the Queen's dominions (i.e., to Ireland), and 'since this travell we have bene both Poeticall, and I Musicall & Pictoricall, & though we may lye and steale by authoritie, yet we are taken for true men, and have holpe to hang theeves.'[4] Harington's Thomas Combe was an educated man, quite capable of literary and artistic activity.

The most direct evidence of these two Thomas Combes being one comes in the conclusion to 'An Anatomie': 'But now, that you may know I have bene a dealer in Emblemes, I will conclude with a devise [in the manuscript this is 'emblem'] not sharpe in conceyt, but of venerable antiquitie . . . Now riddle me what name is this.' The device or rebus for Harington's name that follows is of a hare with a ring in its mouth, standing on a barrel or tun, and encircled by the motto 'Gratia dei nobiscum' (May the grace of God be with us.)

(Reproduced by permission of the Folger Shakespeare Library)

INTRODUCTION

It is accompanied by the verse:

> The (grace of God) guides well both age and youth,
> Fly sin with feare, as harmlesse (hare) doth hound,
> Like precious (ring) embrace, more precious truth,
> As (tunne) full of gold juyce, not emptie sound,
> In these right scand, Mysacmos [i.e. John
>   Harington's] name is found.[5]

Combe is last mentioned in Harington's correspondence in 1608, in a letter to Prince Henry (though it is not clear if Combe is alive at that time),[6] and Harington himself died in 1612.

Text and publishing history

Only two known copies of this rare book are still in existence. That in the Huntington Library bears the date 1614 on its title page and is the only complete copy.[7] This present facsimile edition, however, is based on the incomplete copy in the Stirling Maxwell Collection of the Glasgow University Library, which may be dated c.1593, with the pressmark SM 688. It was formerly in the Nether Pollock collection. Its ideal collation is A-G8 [signed S4], but several pages are missing or damaged: A1 and A2, containing the title page, are missing; only a tiny portion of the text remains along the bound edge of A3, the first leaf of La Perrière's epistle to Marguerite; A4 is torn, with perhaps a quarter of the leaf missing; A5 is very worn along the edge; and G8, containing Emblem 100, is missing entirely.

The two surviving copies of this work represent two different editions. The type has been reset from one to the other, new borders surround the identical woodcuts, and new punctuation and spellings abound. However, only a mere handful of words have been changed – single words such as 'your' to 'our' (no. 83), or 'be old' to 'grow old' (no. 68). These changes are so negligible that authorial participation was certainly not necessary. Other than such minimal alterations, the text is the same in both editions, and in all probability the sections missing from the Glasgow edition were also practically identical to those in the complete 1614 edition. For purposes of comparison, both are reproduced here.

Peter M. Daly has compared these two copies of *The Theater* in 'The Case for the 1593 Edition of Thomas Combe's *Theater of Fine Devices*,' *JWCT* 49 (1986), pp. 255–57 and not only establishes that the Glasgow and Huntington copies are from different editions, but believes that 'there is ample circumstantial evidence to suggest that the first edition did in fact appear in 1593, and that Glasgow's copy is almost certainly from that first edition' (p. 255). This evidence for a 1593 edition consists of Richard Field's entry of

INTRODUCTION

The Theater of Fine Devices in the Stationer's Register on 9 May 1593 (and he only issued two editions of the work of which this is the only record of the first), Combe's reference to himself in the 1596 'Anatomie' as a 'dealer in Emblemes,' Mere's inclusion of Combe's name in his 1598 list of well known emblematists, and the likelihood that several emblems in the 'Four Seasons' tapestries at Hatfield House (with the date 1611 woven into the winter panel) derive from Combe's version of La Perrière's emblems. Sister M. Simon Nolde has pointed out in her 1964 dissertation, 'Whitney's *A Choice of Emblemes* and Three Commonplace Collections of Erasmus' (St. Louis University), that as many as twenty-two quotations from *The Theater* are included among those from a large number of other sources in a commonplace book first published in 1600 and sponsored by John Bodenham, *Belvedere or the Garden of the Muses*. Given the evidence, it is likely that an edition of *The Theater* appeared during the 1590s, probably shortly after Field's registering it in 1593. The Glasgow copy is obviously a different edition from the Huntington's 1614 copy; with no proof of any further editions it seems very likely that the Glasgow copy is from the first, c.1593 edition of *The Theater*.

INTRODUCTION

The Theater as a translation

Combe's translation of Guillaume de la Perrière's *Le Theater des bons engins* into English is, like many other Renaissance translations, a much freer adaptation than twentieth-century readers are accustomed to. Nevertheless, there was no attempt to disguise the translation as an original work; the 1614 title page of *The Theater* announces that the 'hundred morall Emblemes' were 'First penned in French by Guillaume de la Perrière, and translated into English by Thomas Combe'. In all probability the title page of the first edition of *The Theater* carried the same announcement, just as the extant portion of its preface 'To the Reader' speaks of Combe as a translator in terms identical to those in the 1614 edition.

The early publishing history of La Perrière's *La Theatre*, the first emblem book to be published after Alciato's *Emblematum liber* (1531), has been surrounded by confusion. After a careful comparison of various editions, however, Stephen Rawles has come to several conclusions ('The Earliest Editions of Guillaume de la Perrière's *Theatre des bons engins*,' *Emblematica*, 2, no. 2 [Fall 1987] 381–6). An edition with the Daedalus device of the Lyons publisher Denis de Harsy, which is unillustrated but has mottoes, has long been considered the first edition of *Le Theatre* and dated 1536 from the *huytain* at the book's conclusion. (It has no date or publisher's name on title page or colophon.) Rawles convincingly argues that this edition was pirated and postdates the first illustrated edition (Paris: Janot, [1539]). He also establishes that there were four editions with identical woodcut illustrations and without mottoes published in Paris by Denis Janot under the Royal Privilege dated 'le dernier jour de Janvier, mil cinq cents trente neuf' (1539 under old style dating, therefore actually 1540).[8] The third and fourth Janot editions contain many textual changes from the first two, ranging from different wordings in many poems, to changes in the moral lesson (for example in nos. 21 and 43), to the omission of an entire emblem (no. 99), which brings the number of emblems to 100. At least eleven subsequent editions appeared in the next forty-four years, including three editions of a Dutch translation.

A series of editions of *Le Theatre* was published in Lyons from 1545 to 1583 by Jean de Tournes. The large majority of the verses in these editions are the same as in the revised Janot editions, except for variations in spelling and punctuation. In the remaining poems, the changes involve only a word or two and never alter the meaning. Though the verses remain virtually the same, however, the Lyons editions vary from the Paris editions in both picture and motto. Jean de Tournes obviously did not possess Denis Janot's woodcut blocks and commissioned someone, probably Bernard Salomon, who worked for de Tournes during these years, to reproduce them for his editions. They are not exact copies and in some cases are superior to the originals.[9] In addition, one line mottoes or titles are added to the Lyons editions to introduce each emblem. These are not based on the titles in the unillustrated Denis de Harsy edition.

It is evident from my comparisons of the Janot editions of *Le Theatre*, the 1545, the 1553 and 1583 Lyons *Le Theatre*, and Combe's *The Theater* that Combe worked from a Lyons edition.[10] His pictures are very close copies of the Lyons pictures, differing only in minor background details. In only two instances does he modify them to any extent: first in no. 15 where he changes the painting from a full nude to a half-nude, presumably for modesty's sake, and in no. 55 where the fool's cap is turned to feathers. In the one case (no. 51) in which the 1583 verse is significantly altered from the revised Janot edition (the word 'amys' is omitted), Combe follows the 1583 edition. Because of his interest in developing the theme of friendship, it is unlikely Combe would have omitted this from his translation had he seen it. Combe strays further from the Lyons mottoes than from the verse or pictures. The Lyons mottoes are just single line, descriptive titles and are often taken verbatim or with small changes from a line or two of the verse, particularly in the first half of the book. The mottoes of *The Theater* are much more independent of the verse than those in the Lyons *Le Theatre* and form an equal partnership with the picture and verse. Combe's mottoes are no date or publisher's name on title page or colophon.) Rawles convincingly argues that this edition was pirated and postdates the first illustrated edition (Paris: Janot, [1539]). He also establishes that there were four editions with identical woodcut illustrations and without mottoes published in Paris by Denis Janot under the Royal Privilege dated 'le dernier jour de Janvier, mil cinq cents trente neuf' (1539 under old style dating, therefore actually 1540).[8] The third and fourth Janot editions contain many textual changes from the first two, ranging from different wordings in many poems, to changes in the moral lesson (for example in nos. 21 and 43), to the omission of an entire emblem (no. 99), which brings the number of emblems to 100. At least eleven subsequent editions appeared in the next forty-four years, including three editions of a Dutch translation.

A series of editions of *Le Theatre* was published in Lyons from 1545 to 1583 by Jean de Tournes. The large majority of the verses in these editions are the same as in the revised Janot editions, except for variations in spelling and punctuation. In the remaining poems, the changes involve only a word or two and never alter the meaning. Though the verses remain virtually the same, however, the Lyons editions vary from the Paris editions in both picture and motto. Jean de Tournes obviously did not possess Denis Janot's woodcut blocks and commissioned someone, probably Bernard Salomon, who worked for de Tournes during these years, to reproduce them for his editions. They are not exact copies and in some cases are superior to the originals.[9] In addition, one line mottoes or titles are added to the Lyons editions to introduce each emblem. These are not based on the titles in the unillustrated Denis de Harsy edition.

It is evident from my comparisons of the Janot editions of *Le Theatre*, the 1545, the 1553 and 1583 Lyons *Le Theatre*, and Combe's *The Theater* that Combe worked from a Lyons edition.[10] His pictures are very close copies of the Lyons pictures, differing only in minor background details. In only two instances does he modify them to any extent: first in no. 15 where he changes the painting from a full nude to a half-nude, presumably for modesty's sake, and in no. 55 where the fool's cap is turned to feathers. In the one case (no. 51) in which the 1583 verse is significantly altered from the revised Janot edition (the word 'amys' is omitted), Combe follows the 1583 edition. Because of his interest in developing the theme of friendship, it is unlikely Combe would have omitted this from his translation had he seen it. Combe strays further from the Lyons mottoes than from the verse or pictures. The Lyons mottoes are just single line, descriptive titles and are often taken verbatim or with small changes from a line or two of the verse, particularly in the first half of the book. The mottoes of *The Theater* are much more independent of the verse than those in the Lyons *Le Theatre* and form an equal partnership with the picture and verse. Combe's mottoes are usually unlike La Perrière's, but in a few instances he picks up a word or idea (for example, in nos. 17, 23, 46, 67, and 73) found within the French motto but not the verse, which suggests he had the Lyons motto in front of him.

Combe's translation is usually quite faithful to La Perrière's sense and often even to his wording, though qualified by a different language and verse form. About a third of the emblems are not significantly changed. They are more or less straightforward translations, not word for word, but faithfully using the French poem as a guide. Combe makes changes to the remaining emblems, however, that give his *Theater* a character quite distinct from that of *Le Theatre*, while still remaining a translation.

Critical discussion

Combe begins by closely translating La Perrière's epistle dedicated to Marguerite de Navarre, which excuses the small number of emblems, apparently only fifty when he presented them to her on her visit to Toulouse in 1535. La Perrière also gives a brief history of emblems, tracing them from the hicroglyphical 'figures and images' of the Egyptians and acknowledging his own imitation of Alciato. The unsigned preface 'To the Reader' which is then added to the

English translation explains the special moral value of emblems, comprising as they do both word and picture:

> The more (gentle Reader) the conceit is pierced with the substance and life of that which anie way is objected, the more we endevour to embrace or eschue the good or evill the object or subject proposeth. So that where oftentimes feeling and effectuall words, though never so sensible, passe the Reader without due consideration; pictures that especially are discerned by the sense, are such helpes to the weaknesse of common understandings, that they make words as it were deeds, and set the whole substance of that which is offered before the sight and conceipt of the Reader. (sig. A5)

Emblems here have a special ability to possess the senses and persuade the will – a claim familiar to anyone acquainted with Renaissance poetic theory. According to this preface, *The Theater* is something of a sixteenth century self-help book, aiding the reader to achieve the virtuous and prudent life. Each motto is a succinct introduction of the lesson to be learned from the picture and poem. The picture then gives the metaphoric form of the emblem which, as Combe explains in his epistle, he hopes will pierce the reader more effectively than words alone. The verse acts to reinforce the moral through explanation of the visual image and further examples.

INTRODUCTION

Combe then proceeds to translate and adapt La Perrière's one hundred emblems. Each of Combe's emblems has three parts: an *inscriptio* of a couplet of iambic tetrameter, a *pictura* surrounded by one of the two border patterns Field used in this edition, and a *subscriptio* composed of a stanza of ottava rima. A close look at the first emblem will be useful since it not only sets the tone for the remaining emblems, following the lead of the preface, but also gives us an idea of how Combe manages both to translate and yet also to add his own interpretation. The title for Emblem 1, 'Pour vivre en paix & en tranquillité,' is simply adopted from the last line of its dizain, 'Qu'il pourra vivre en grand tranquillité.' It has none of the riddling quality of Combe's, 'According to the time forepast, / Be wisely warned of the last,' which contains the emblem's message in a form only to be completely understood by the combined revelations of the picture and verse. The word 'paix' in this 1583 title is picked up by Combe and used in the conclusion to his verse, while Combe's picture is a close copy of the Lyons picture, though he alters the building in the background slightly and adds a couple of birds in the sky. The English verse carefully preserves the subject of the original and the significance of Janus's double face, and even key words such as 'providence' and 'Vertu' are carried over. But Combe changes it slightly, adding his own touches. Where La Perrière merely says that wise men look to the future as well as the past, Combe says the wise *should* remember the past in order to foresee the future, altering his emphasis from observing behaviour to influencing it. La Perrière relies on the authority of 'Nos anciens' to carry his observation; Combe eliminates this reference. Furthermore, the phrasing that Combe uses in several places adds a suggestion that this desired and wise behaviour is, for him, rooted in the Christian religion. While La Perrière simply concludes that by such means one can live in tranquillity, Combe concludes that the wise who embrace virtue 'Themselves to rest and quite peace shal bring.' A spiritual interpretation for this line is supported by the phrase 'at the last' in the English motto and by the biblical reference (1 Cor 9:24) which Combe adds to line 5, 'And with such providence direct their race,' not found in the French original. Throughout his emblem book Combe continues this process of combining translation and adaptation.

The process extends to Combe's treatment of La Perrière's themes. Following in the steps of Alciato, La Perrière and Combe explore a wide range of subjects and themes, usually aspects of the social and political world – to name a few, government and the relations between ruler and ruled, behaviour at court, corruption and the abuse of privilege, vices and the need for temperance in both pleasures and griefs, love, women, friendship, time, the need to know oneself and one's abilities, hypocrisy, the inadvisability of relying on fortune, and raising children. Most of these themes remain largely unchanged in the translation because they are as much a concern to Combe's audience as to La Perrière's. Combe retains, for example, five of the six instances of La Perrière's direct advice to rulers (LP 22, 45, 50, 53, 54, 92; C 22, 50, 53, 54, 92). Combe's advice on women (2, 16, 18, 37, 78, 88, 96), love (62, 77, 79, 80, 81), and marriage (93) is the same as La Perrière's. Some themes, though, Combe does transform. A number of the French emblems on the abuse of privilege and the ill-treatment of educated men are strongly satirical and are altered in Combe's general lessening of the satiric cast of La Perrière's work. He also restructures La Perrière's strongly linked themes of hypocrisy and court life so that in the English version hypocrisy becomes tied to the theme of friendship, which Combe augments at the expense of the theme of court life.[11]

Changes such as these seem to be aimed at adapting *The Theater* to its new audience, one that was not only English but also apparently from a lower social order than La Perrière's. La Perrière (c.1499–1553) was a native of Toulouse, headmaster of a school, historiographer of his city, a prolific writer, and creator of four emblem books. A scholar, he associated with other scholars and poets.[12] Combe, on the other hand, was a servant, albeit an educated and well placed one. Where La Perrière's dedication hopes the emblems will please a princess (although the reference to Alciato implies a general usefulness too), Combe's preface explains how well suited emblems are for helping 'the weaknesse of common understandings,' and it expresses the hope that the translator's work was 'worthily bestowed' in providing 'precepts and rebukes to our behaviours,' 'for instruction sake.' In order to accommodate these 'common understandings' Combe cuts the number of La Perrière's scholarly allusions (for example, to Pythagoras or Homer) by half. Instead of these references he carefully identifies iconographic or classical figures and adds the traditional attributes usually associated with them. Fortune regains her wheel (nos. 20, 28), Baccus his flagon and bowl (no. 48), and Bucephalus is identified as Alexander's horse (no. 91).

As a work concerned with contemporary social behaviour, *Le Theater* has a definite moral cast. This attitude is not only carried into the English translation, but is intensified to become the major characteristic of *The Theater*. Combe emphasizes each emblem's moral lesson and advice to the individual, even when it means he has to alter some of his translations from La Perrière's originally satiric or observational poems. He often, for example, increases the number of lines devoted to direct advice for action, even though his poems are two lines shorter than La Perrière's – this in addition to the direct advice given in each English motto. In Emblem 4, for example, Combe discards the dance image that could diffuse the moral point (LP lines 7–8), and instead he gives the reader four lines of instruction rather than La Perrière's two. In other instances Combe emphasizes the moral of a poem by changing La Perrière's mode of question or observation to assertion; La Perrière's version of no. 12 is an amused observation, balanced by a series of questions, on the rashness of youth and the fearfulness of old age, while Combe's is largely a straightforward criticism and warning against youth's excesses.

Combe's concern for extracting as much moral teaching from each emblem as possible is exhibited time and again in his changes to La Perrière's text. In no. 87, for example, he completely alters La Perrière's celebration of the poet's glory to a reminder that the reader must select the correct moral from any verse that he reads. In no. 65 he retains La Perrière's general subject and even wording, but makes slight changes that direct the reader to mend his own life rather than to test other men's reputations as La Perrière recommends. Always keeping in mind his role as moral instructor, Combe balances La Perrière's discussion of the need for ease from work in no. 25 (the picture is of a bow drawn too long) with a reminder that the opposite extreme is also bad: 'For sloth corrupts and duls our might & strength,/ But too much toyling breeds a greater sore.' Combe often changes La Perrière's worldly advice or observations to moral advice, as in no. 36 where Combe adjusts La Perrière's political or social comment on the difficulty of curing entrenched abuses to a personal level. Similarly, in no. 59 Combe generalizes La Perrière's business advice to fit any situation in which immediate action is needed rather than creating greater dangers by delay.

Combe's aim – 'education' rather than biting condemnation – is served by redirecting several of La Perrière's emblems from satire to moral counsel by removing exaggerated or grotesque descriptions (eg, 13, 40, 75), or by removing the attack on a specific group such as the clergy in no. 13 or judges in no. 66. His renaming of the antagonist in no. 100 from Famine to Idleness redirects the emblem's focus from a problem beyond the control of the reader to something within his control and correctable. *Le Theater* shows La Perrière's preoccupation with the problems of the educated but unrewarded man; he sees life from the perspective of the learned (eg, in nos. 13, 15, 17, 19, 29, 46, 50, 64, 69, 85). Combe changes the impetus of this group of emblems to a concern that all attend to virtue and education. He does not change their subject; for example, fools are still rewarded before wise men in nos 13 and 46, but he widens their application to include all readers. Where La Perrière refers the reader to St. Paul in no. 15 and warns that one should only strive to know enough, not too much, Combe omits the reference to St. Paul and concludes that those who search too far into 'things most divine' 'do not know themselves so as they ought.' He thus ends our need to know ourselves rather than limiting our knowledge – a positive goal for the ordinary individual rather than a warning for the learned few.

We can trace the influence of Alciato on perhaps ten emblems in *Le Theatre*, and in a number of emblems La Perrière tells us his source. The general influence of Horapollo's *Hieroglyphica*, the Greek Anthology, and commonplace books such as Erasmus's *Adages* on emblems books is well known. However, the sources of inspiration for La Perrière's and Combe's emblems are widespread. La Perrière borrowed from classical sources for stories, ancient authorities, and figures such as Bacchus (eg, nos. 8, 26, 48, 57, 99). Natural history, and the often unnatural history of Pliny, the bestiaries, and fables acount for a large number of the emblems (eg, nos. 28, 34, 47, 61, 69, 97, 98). Iconographical figures (eg, nos. 18, 20, 29, 63, 100) and tales of odd doings in other places appear in several emblems as well (13, 75). The largest group, however, are examples from everyday life, often proverbial (eg, nos. 4, 7, 33, 37, 46, 53, 74, 81, 85).

Since this emblem book is concerned with everyday behaviour, we get something of a picture of everyday life at the time. So we have tennis playing in 41 and 5, masking in 6, chess and another board game in 27 and 59, eel fishing 44, medicine 50, fowling 54, dishonest lawyers 66, a still 79, gardening 81; the list could go on. This area is where a number of the changes in translation appear as Combe alters French customs and idioms to English equivalents. A difference in the diet of French and English pigs, for example, is duly noted in no. 24. While La Perrière's pig receives 'le gland' (acorn) as his proper share, Combe maintains 'decorum' by giving 'draffe' to his. In a similar move Combe specifies that the ivy-choked tree that La Perrière leaves anonymous (82) is an oak. 'Roger bon temps' becomes 'Robin Good-fellow' (29), and a reference to the barbaric Goths is omitted from no. 69. Social differences also account for some of the changes Combe made. La Perrière's topic of the abuses of pilgrimage in no. 51 was not appropriate for Protestant England, and Combe alters it to emphasize the need for the old to stay at home, the topic of the Lyons motto. Combe makes a subtle change to La Perrière's no. 22: while La Perrière emphasizes the war-like accomplishments of the prince who, 'comme vray chef de guerre,' must combine the attributes of lion and fox 'Si triumpher veut par mer, & par terre,' Combe retains the emblem's subject of the need for the prince to be both crafty and courageous if he wishes to 'purchase endlesse fame,' but no mention is made of war.

Not only does Combe change La Perrière's moral and thematic concerns, he also modifies the structure and style of the verse. The three-part form of Combe's emblems works well. Combe's mottoes were planned from the beginning rather than the afterthought that La Perrière's obviously were, and they therefore seem to balance better with the other two sections of each emblem.

The verse of *The Theater* possesses some of the best qualities of didactic poetry. It is generally clear, easy and pleasing – characteristics often missing in sixteenth-century didactic verse – and frequently strikes one with an apt epigrammatic phrase. These qualities are partially due to the rigours of his chosen verse form, ottava rima, whose strictures forced Combe into a compact sententiousness. The rhyme scheme – abababcc – of ottava rima places a fairly heavy demand on a poet writing in English. Developed in thirteenth and fourteenth-century Italy, ottava rima was the dominant form of Italian narrative verse and reached its finest development in Ariosto's *Orlando Furioso* (1516), which Harington translated around the time that Combe would presumably have been translating *Le Theater*. Ottava rima was introduced into England by Wyatt and was used by Sidney, Spenser, Harington, and Drayton. Because of its concluding couplet it is well suited to a culminating epigrammatic assessment of its subject. Perhaps Combe's choice of verse form, quite different from La Perrière's *dizain*, can be credited to the influence of Harington, a well known epigrammatist of Elizabeth's court.

The attractiveness of *The Theater* derives from more than

Combe's usually confident handling of his versification. The work has an appealingly informal and lively tone, produced through its manipulation of the epigrammatic possibilities of the motto and ottava rima, his plain diction interspersed with colloquial and sprightly descriptions, his English proverbs, and his concrete imagery. So what could have been a heavily and self importantly didactic work is made enjoyable by these qualities.

Combe makes great use of the epigrammatic possibilities in ottava rima, both for succinct statement and for an air of informality. He often alters the structure or line arrangement of La Perrière's verse in order to take advantage of the form's capacity for succinct statement and informal tone, especially at the couplet conclusion (eg, nos. 9, 19, 26, 40, 62, 66, 77). He reorganizes no. 66, for example, so that he not only concludes with the striking image of the lawyer's hands full of eyes, found at the opening of La Perrière's verse, but also shapes his couplet into a comprehensive epigram on the subject of the hypocrisy of lawyers.

Combe's choice of plain diction is possibly a matter of decorum.

The line 'Such one with heed, and grave & good instruction' (no. 4) is simple but succeeds in matching verse technique to content as Combe attempts to make the reader pause and think before ruining his life with vain pleasures. The rhythm of iambic pentameter adds to this understated style. Combe's plain diction is continually leavened by figures of speech such as alliteration and by his felicitous phrasing and vigorous word choices. In no. 71, La Perrière prosily squanders four lines explaining that one is not permitted to consume time in great revelry: if you lose it, it will not be possible for you to recover such a precious thing. Combe translates this message in only two lines as, 'For those that leade their lives in belly-cheare, / Do leese their time, of al things else most deare.' Combe creates a great sense of animation in no. 43 by opening with a vivid description of the blustery winds and the 'merrie shore,' continuing with a series of questions that mimic the action of searching for alternatives, and closing with an energetic proverb – none of which are in La Perrière. All this enhances the emblem's topic of trying to rouse the defeated to yet another attempt.

Colloquial diction is also used by Combe to great effect. It is inevitable that something will be lost in any translation, particularly on the level of word play and idiomatic expression. There is, for example, no English equivalent for the forceful and ironic French conclusion to no. 75, in which the malefactors will be installed 'comme evesques des champs' (like bishops of the fields), ie, hanged. Combe's conclusion is much less effective without this idiomatic vigour. Similarly Combe cannot reproduce the French pun on 'cerf' (deer, stag) and 'serf' in no. 39.[13] Combe more than makes up for these occasional losses, however, and invests *The Theater* with its own style and spirit. He often adds an informal or mocking touch to his translation by applying English idiomatic expressions to disparage undesirable behaviour. This is not a technique used by La Perrière. Thus, the proud men at court in Combe's no. 42 are described as those 'that can cog and foist with all the rout.' The impatient man in no. 55 unsuccessfully strives with 'might and main,' but merely proves his resemblance to the proverbially 'foolish furious dawes.' The motto of no. 85 gives, in unmistakable terms, Combe's opinion of the man who strives for the impossible: 'Who labours that to bring to passe,/ That cannot be, is but an Asse.' And in no. 93, where La Perrière gravely advises a man to choose his wife not by his eye or hand, but by his ear (ie, by her reputation), Combe mocks the man who would choose for the wrong reason by the slang with which he describes marrying for money: 'Others so they be fingring of the chinke, / Care not how soone their hand be in the pie.'.

Combe's use of proverbs also differs from La Perrière's and reflects his interest in stressing ethical teachings and his different class of audience. Many of La Perrière's emblems are themselves based on proverbs: the swine that prefers the mud to precious balms in no. 17, the rose's thorns in nos. 19 and 30, the eagle and flies in no. 32, and the impossibility of catching the wind in no. 36. But while La

Perrière never uses additional proverbs in his mottoes and very rarely in his verse, Combe relies heavily on them. In four instances he draws attention to his proverbs by naming them as such (nos. 3, 10, 20, 71), he replaces French proverbs with English ones (77, 82, 88), and he regularly uses additional proverbs (eg, in 5, 9, 30, 43, 53, 55, 84, 88) to reinforce the lesson of the central emblem image. While we see blindfolded Fortune leading a blindfolded man in the *pictura* to no. 20, Combe verbally reminds us that 'When blind do leade the blind, they both do lye / In ditch, the Proverbe saith.'.

On the whole, the French version is more prosaic, while Combe's images serve both to enliven the work and to direct it to an English audience. Combe rounds off the clothing image of no. 53 with the proverbial line: 'As in fine cloth the brightest staines we see.' The enemy of the virtuous man in no. 89 comes to life when personified: 'Though envy brag, & thogh she draw her blade.'. La Perrière simply and drily establishes his comparison of the constant man with the steadfast anvil in his opening two lines to no. 67. The rest of his verse is an abstract recommendation of the virtue. Combe, however, vividly exploits the physical immediacy of the smithy in which the anvil 'endures the heavie hammers beat' while the 'smiths lay on & thump it till they sweat'.

Combe develops a series of sailing images not found in La

INTRODUCTION

Perrière: in no. 14 and in the motto to no. 28, Combe adds a sailing image in order to bring to life the virtue of constancy in friendship and in opposing the vagaries of fortune. In no. 97 he goes so far as to replace La Perrière's perfectly functional image of constancy as a bulwark against adversity with the more active and expressive image of constancy as a sailing ship which does not just oppose the wind, but actually gains strength from it, in the same way that the constant wind gains strength from adversity.

Combe and Whitney

Emblematists often borrowed from each other, and many, if not most, English emblem books rely upon Continental sources, especially for the pictorial elements of their emblems. The inter-relationships among emblem books reveal both their imitation and invention as each author strives to make the material his own. Though Combe was translating La Perrière, his care in adapting *La Theatre* caused him to look at Geffrey Whitney's adaptations from La Perrière for changes pertinent to Combe's own work.

Geffrey Whitney (1548–1603) appropriated nine emblems from La Perrière's *Le Theatre*, along with those from several other continental emblem books, for his *A Choice of Emblemes* published in Leiden in 1586.[14] Whitney was mainly interested in the pictures from *Le Theatre* and created his own English verse and Latin mottoes to accompany them, either drawing a different subject from La Perrière from the same picture (W 108, 179, and partially 208; LP 1, 70 and 59) or expanding and diversifying the subject so greatly that his verse owes practically nothing to the French verse (W 165, 175, 180, 188a, 192, 205; LP 30, 100, 90, 47, 31, 65). Whitney's pictures, very similar to Combe's, are close copies of a de Tournes edition of *Le Theatre*.

Combe appears to have consulted Whitney's book when preparing his translation of *Le Theatre*, but there does not seem to be a pattern to his use of it.[15] In some cases he pays no attention to Whitney, whether Whitney retains La Perrière's subject (W192, LP31; W180, LP90) or not (W108, LP1), or even when Combe also strays from La Perrière (W208, LP59). In a couple of instances Combe translates La Perrière quite closely, but borrows a word or two from Whitney (W165, C30; W205, C65); for example, Combe may have adopted the word 'barren' from Whitney's no. 205, and he apparently could not resist the pairing of sweet and sour from Whitney's expansion of La Perrière's no. 30.

Combe's borrowing is a little more extensive in no. 100 (W175). The triumphant figure in Combe's verse is called Diligence, as in La Perrière, but she is 'wroth' (possibly suggested by Whitney's 'Ire') and sits in a 'charriot' (as in

Whitney's description), 'with a scourge in hand, / And whippeth Idleness' (Whitney says labour 'whippes' Idleness). Like Whitney, Combe calls the second figure 'Idlenesse' rather than La Perrière's Famine. Combe ends, like Whitney, with a more austere moral than La Perrière, while his motto carries the less elemental message of La Perrière's conclusion. The changes in this emblem reflect Combe's general practice of altering La Perrière's text to emphasize how the individual reader can reform himself. In this case, it is within the individual's power to defeat the figure of Idleness which Combe borrowed from Whitney, but never La Perrière's Famine.

In only one case does Combe change the theme of his emblem to align more closely with Whitney's (W179, C70), but even here Combe in no way slavishly follows him. The theme of La Perrière's no. 70 is the danger of following the court in hopes of earthly honours. Combe alters his theme to Whitney's more widely applicable one: the dangers one will endure for riches. The relationship between the picture (of a burdened, swimming man) and the verse in which this emblem becomes progressively less metaphoric from La Perrière, to Combe, to Whitney. While Whitney speaks directly of the shipwrecked merchant who will endanger his life by swimming with a burden, Combe criticizes any man who will endanger himself for mere worldly goods. Both Whitney and Combe use the word 'venture'; Whitney speaks of the 'thirst of goulde,' Combe of the 'thirst for worldly goods.'

In a unique case (W188a, C47) Combe appears to have adopted some changes from Whitney's text, even though Whitney's picture of a monkey holding its crushed baby is actually from Paradin's *Symbola Heroica*. It is therefore not precisely the same as in La Perrière and Combe, although it is similar and the theme is the same for all four emblematists. Combe seems to have been influenced by Whitney's version of this emblem on rearing children to change La Perrière's male monkey to a female, and fathers to parents. This alteration underlines the care Combe took in translating creatively. A female is more likely to care for the young, and the word 'parents' rather than 'fathers' widens the application of the lesson, perhaps an indication that Combe was more consciously including women in his audience. These last three instances of more substantial modifications that Combe adopted from Whitney reinforce Combe's now familiar programme for adapting La Perrière's emblems. What is emphasized is a moral lesson which can be absorbed and practised by the widest possible audience.

INTRODUCTION

Conclusion

Combe's work in translating *Le Theatre* has not been fully appreciated and, to all intents and purposes, it has been lost to modern readers – a fate his lively and well written translation does not deserve. Though obviously more of a translation than Whitney's emblem book, *The Theater* is still quite definitely an English emblem book marked with Combe's own preoccupations and style. His command of the emblem form, of its subtleties and moral power, is clear. Each emblem is an integrated whole which not only realizes Combe's own concept of what an emblem should be, as found in his preface, but also fulfils another popular view of the emblem. Many theorists derived the term 'emblem' from the Greek ἔμβλημα, meaning mosaic or inlay. In a mosaic each piece is complete in itself, but is also a necessary part of a greater whole. In Combe's emblems each part – motto, picture, and verse – works with the others to create a vivid and forceful moral statement. And each emblem forms one small piece of Combe's varied theatre of the prudent and virtuous life.

Although we cannot know for certain Combe's contemporary success, we do know that demand for his first edition was great enough to induce Field to go to the expense of printing a new edition some twenty years later. The influence of *The Theater* on the Hatfield tapestries and on the commonplace book, *Belvedere*, leads one to suspect that, as it becomes better known, more references may well be found. Combe's book deserves a place in any study of the English emblem tradition and its impact on the literature and culture of the period.

Mary V. Silcox
University of Nova Scotia

Note on type-page measurement of original [SM 688]:
F1^r: 88 mm (111 with headline and direction line) x 70 mm.

Notes

Some portions of this introduction are substantially the same as in my article 'The Translation of La Perrière's *Le Theatre des bons engins* into Combe's *The Theater of Fine Devices*,' *Emblematica*, 2 (1987), pp. 61–94, and are reproduced courtesy of *Emblematica*.

INTRODUCTION

[1] Elizabeth Story Donno, 'Introduction,' to *Sir John Harington's A New Discourse of a Stale Subject, Called the Metamorphosis of Ajax*, London: Routledge & Kegan Paul, 1962, p. 13. All further quotations from the *Metamorphosis* are from this edition. Guy Butler has suggested that the Thomas Combe who translated *Le Theatre* was Thomas Combe, senior, of Stratford-upon-Avon's leading family and well known to Shakespeare; 'Shakespeare's Cliff at Dover and an Emblem Illustration,' *Huntington Library Quarterly*, 47 (1984), 226–31. The evidence he presents for his conclusion is, however, rather slim: the coincidence of names and the fact that the publisher Richard Field originally came from Stratford and printed both *Venus and Adonis* and *The Theater*.

[2] Harington opens the letter, 'Good Thomas, I have received sundry letters from you . . . In sundry of your letters, I have received good advertisement and honest counsels, and great good wishes, all which I take in good part.' He later says he has been 'reading the book you so prays'd.' He acknowledges Combe's letters: 'gentle Thomas, I have, in recompence of your long letters, enlarged the discourse of my Irish affairs' and closes calling him 'friend Thomas'. *The Letters and Epigrams of Sir John Harington*, edited and introduced by Norman Egbert McClure, Philadelphia: University of Pennsylvania Press, 1930, pp. 71–76.

[3] Combe in Harington's *Metamorphosis*, p. 190. In her notes Donno suggests that this could be an allusion to Harington's brother Francis who attended Oxford. John Harington went to Cambridge.

[4] Combe in Harington's *Metamorphosis*, pp. 203–3. Donno glosses the line 'we may lye and steal by authoritie' with: 'In reference to the fact that both Harington and Combe's published works were translations. Cf. Harington's epigram "Of honest Theft. To my good friend Master Samuel Daniel".' This epigram is to be found in Harington's *Letters and Epigrams*, p. 196.

[5] Combe in Harington's *Metamorphosis*, p. 204. Harington published the *Metamorphosis* under the pseudonym Misacmos. In the presentation copy now at the Folger Shakespeare Library, Harington annotated the riddle and explained that this first name, John, means 'the grace of God'.

[6] *Letters and Epigrams*, p. 132.

[7] The Hungtington Library published a facsimile edition of this 1614 copy in 1983 with a brief introduction by John Doebler.

[8] The first illustrated edition of *Le Theatre* was reproduced by Scolar Press, in 1973, ed. by John Horden, Introductory Note by Alison Saunders. The third, revised Janot edition has also been published in facsimile, by Scholars' Facsimiles & Reprints, Delmar, New York, 1964,

with an Introduction by Greta Dexter. The Lyons editions have unfortunately not been reproduced in a modern edition.

[9] For information on Salomon and his work for Jean de Tournes, see M. Natalis Rondot, *Bernard Salomon: Peintre et Tailleur d'Histoires à Lyon, au XVIe Siècle*, Lyons: Mougin-Rusand, 1897, pp. 24, 66ff.; and Jean Adhémar, *Inventaire du Fonds Français: Graveurs de Seizième Siècle*, vol. 2, Paris: Bibliothèque Nationale, 1971, pp. 95–101.

[10] My conclusions about the Lyons editions are based on an examination of the 1545 *Le Theatre* at the Herzog August Bibliothek in Wolfenbüttel, the 1553 *Le Theatre* at Princeton, and the 1583 *Le Theatre* at the University of Illinois. All three editions have the same woodcuts, and their mottoes and epigrams vary in only minor ways. It is unlikely that other Lyons editions would stray from these three.

[11] See my article, listed at the beginning of these notes, for a more complete discussion of this change.

[12] For a more complete biography of La Perrière, see Saunders's and Dexter's introductions to the facsimile editions of *Le Theatre* listed in n.8 and Dexter's note 'Guillaume de la Perrière' in *Bibliothèque d'Humanisme et Renaissance*, vol. 17, Geneva: Droz, 1955, pp. 56–73.

[13] Michael Bath, 'Collared Stags and Bridled Lions: Queen Elizabeth's Household Accounts,' in Peter M. Daly,

ed., *The English Emblem and the Continental Tradition*, New York: AMS Press, 1988, p. 229.

[14] References to Whitney are from Henry Green's edition of *A Choice of Emblemes*, London: 1866; rpt. New York: Benjamin Blom, 1967, Mason Tung's article, 'Whitney's *A Choice of Emblemes* Revisited: A Comparative Study of the Manuscript and the Printed Versions,' *Studies in Bibliography*, 29 (1976), supersedes Green's essay on the nature of Whitney's debt to various emblematists.

[15] Combe evidently consulted the published version of *Choice*, not the manuscript. From Harington's 'Advertisement' to his translation of *Orlando Furioso* it is known that he had seen the published *Choice* by 1591 – presumably so had his servant Combe. Furthermore, in the one instance in which a manuscript emblem by Whitney which was modelled on La Perrière was not carried over into his published edition (W ms 91b; LP 6), there is no resemblance between Whitney's verse and Combe's.

Further reading

Butler, Guy. 'Shakespeare's Cliff at Dover and an Emblem Illustration,' *Huntington Library Quarterly*, 47 (1984), 226–31.

INTRODUCTION

Daly, Peter M. 'The Case for the 1593 Edition of Thomas Combe's *Theater of Fine Devices*,' *Journal of the Warburg and Courtaulds Institutes*, 49 (1986), 255–57.

Doebler, John. Preface and Introduction to Thomas Combe's *The Theater of Fine Devices*. San Marino, Cal.: The Huntington Library, 1983.

Donno, Elizabeth Story, ed. and intro. *Sir John Harington's A New Discourse of a Stale Subject, Called the Metamorphosis of Ajax*. London: Routledge & Kegan Paul, 1962.

Kirwood, A.E.M. 'Richard Field, Printer, 1589–1624,' *The Library*, fourth series, vol. 12, no. 1 (1931), 1–39.

Nolde, Sister M. Simon. 'Whitney's *A Choice of Emblemes* and Three Commonplace Collections of Erasmus.' Diss. St. Louis University, 1964.

Silcox, Mary V. 'The Translation of La Perrière's *La Theatre des bons engins* into Combe's *The Theater of Fine Devices*,' *Emblematica*, 2 (1987), 61–94.

This very curious volume of English Emblems printed about 1591 is absolutely unique & hitherto unknown

cen
fu
re
i
s

om-
epare
s, ac-
eries,
their
e to
our
ow-
s)
ri-
I
.   I
ng
ut
ly
ſ-
:

hath not bene to m...
Wherefore considering
my selfe, I do presume
vnto your Maiestie my sa
though they haue attained
number that I intended; B
Maiestie to receiue them (suc
according to your accustomed b
and that with so good wil as they a
your poore seruant offered and pre
Moreouer (Madame) it is not onely
time that Emblemes are in accout & sin
lar regard, but it hath bin of ancient ti
& almost frō the beginning of the worl
the Egyptians (which thinke themsel
be the first people of the world) befo
vse of letters, wrote by figures an
as well of men, beasts, fowles a
of serpents; thereby expressing
ons, as is written by most an
Chæremon, *Orus*, *Apollo*, and th
haue laboured diligently and
expound the said hieroglyp

...keth mention in
...le the author of the
...ription of his dreame,
...his Commentaries of
...*Alciat* hath likewise in
...certaine Emblemes, and
...with Latine verses. And I
...these abouesaid) esteeme the
...bestowed, which I employed in
...ing and beautifying of these said
...es: and I shall thinke my selfe most
...if the reading hereof may yeeld you
...onest recreation: praying God (most
...ble Princesse) that he will send you
long life, and euerlasting
happinesse.

Your humble seruant,

Guillaume de la Perriere.

To the Reader.

He more (gentle Reader) th[e]
conceit is pierced with the
substance and life of th[at]
which anie way is obiect[ed]
the more we endeuour to e[m]
brace or eschue the good or euill the obie[ct]
or subiect proposeth. So that where ofte[n]
times feeling and effectuall words, thoug[h]
neuer so sensible, passe the Reader witho[ut]
due consideration; pictures that especially ar[e]
discerned by the sense, are such helpes to th[e]
weaknesse of common vnderstandings, th[at]
they make words as it were deeds, an[d]
the whole substance of that which i[s]

To the Reader.

...ed before the sight and conceipt of the Reader. Therefore for instruction sake is his labour worthily bestowed, that vndertooke and accomplished the Translation of this book: containing precepts and rebukes to our behauiors.

Wherein if the verse be anie thing obscure, the impreses or pictures make it more liuely, and in a manner actuall. For the credite and acceptation of it, let the estimation which it had in the French, suffice to grace and commend it Englished: being dedicated vnto the Queene of Nauarre, whose dignitie should not haue beene presented with a worke of any small value: which suppositions and authorities though they make it nothing the better, yet serue they very vvorthily to moue thy desire to the tryall of the Contents, both by seeing and reading them: wherein let not the common conceit of the world withdraw thy minde, which hates any thing that is bitter to their flattering delights:

To the Reader.

lights: but moued with thine owne profite, and helpe of thy better part, requite the Translators paines in reading and obseruing, and thou shalt double his deserts in thine owne profit.

EMBLEME I.

According to the time forepast,
Be wisely warned at the last.

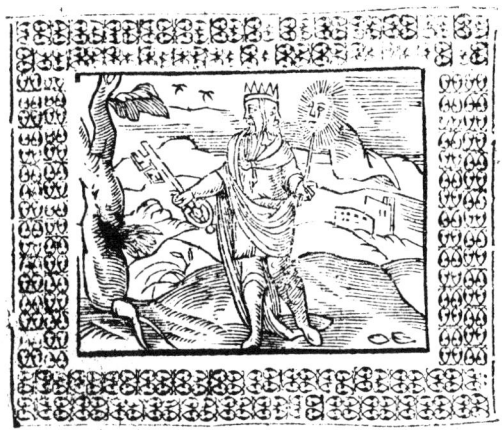

Ianus is figur'd with a double face,
To note at once the time to come and past:
So should the wise obserue the passed space,
As they may well foresee a chance at last:
And with such prouidence direct their race,
That in their thoughts both times be euer plaste.
  Embracing vertue then in euery thing,
    Themselues to rest and quiet peace shal bring.

Ven'rie and drinke do now and then
Besot some of the wisest men.

We reade when *Bacchus* faire dame *Venus* met,
They two together walked forth in chase,
Forthwith their engines and their snares they set,
T'intrap the next that should come in the place:
And straight *Minerua* taken in their net,
Was holden prisner in a wofull case.

By which is shewne, as we may plaine perceiue,
That wine and women wisest folkes deceiue.

EMBLEME I.I

Who doth presume aboue his state,
Doth still incurre the greater hate.

Thou that in court doest spend thy merry dayes,
Sport not with Princes, if that thou be wise:
For he that with his owne superiours playes,
Shall find great perils thereof to arise.
Meddle with thy match, the anciēt prouerb says:
On equall play-fellowes no danger lies.
  He that presumes to shaue the Lions skin
  Full little knowes what danger he is in

EMBLEME IIII.

In pleasures vaine no time bestow,
Lest it procure your ouerthrow.

The Flie so often to the milk-pan vseth,
That in sweet milke at last her death she taketh:
The foole delights in pleasures that he chuseth,
So long vntill his ruine he awaketh.
But happie he who so in time refuseth,
And all vaine fancies vtterly forsaketh: (ction
  Such one with heed, and graue & good instru-
  Doth wisely shun his perill and destruction.

EMBLEME V.

One bird in hand is better farre,
Then three that in the hedges arre.

Who doth expect the bals vncertaine bound,
And quite permit the certaine flight go by,
A player bad at tennis he is found,
And gets but seldome any good thereby.
So some neglect the true and perfect ground,
And for vaine hope do wander quite awry,
  That with fond enterprises and vaine glory,
  With diuers troubles haue thēselues made sory.

EMBLEME V.

Most men do vse some colour'd shift,
For to conceale their crafty drift.

Masks will be more hereafter in request,
And grow more deare than they did heretofore
They seru'd then onely but in play and iest,
For merriment, and to no purpose more:
Now be they vsde in earnest of the best,
And of such maskers there abound such store,
   That you shall find but few in any place,
   That carrie not sometimes a double face.

B

He that doth loue to liue at ease,
An angry man must not displease.

Who will with sword be soding of the fire,
Must looke to haue the sparkes flie in his face:
They that delight with speech as sharpe as brire
To choler others with an humour base,
Vnlooked for perhaps shall find retire,
Words or else deeds, vnto their owne disgrace:
   He that will stirre the angrie man thats still,
   Assure himselfe, his hands shall quickly fill.

EMBLEME VII.

It were a foolish senslesse part,
With griefe and care to eate thy hart.

The wise *Pythagoras* hath euer taught,
Man should not eate vp his owne proper hart,
Nor as a stranger to himselfe be brought
To wast his life with sorrow and with smart,
But so himselfe to temper still he ought,
That woes and cares may vanish from each part:
  Sith nothings hinders more a mans wel-fare,
  Then lingring sorrow, heauinesse and care.

EMBLEME IX.

There be some fooles the cords do spin,
Wherein themselues be netted in.

Who striues to set a narrow ring and straight
Vpon his finger, which too grosse he finds,
Like to the foole that bytes at eu'ry bayt,
Himselfe with his owne folly often binds.
While for felicitie some thinke they wayt,
They fall in bondages of diuerse kinds:
 But wise men vse their fortitu[d]e to shunne
 Such scruitude as fooles into do [r]unne.

EMBLEME

Vse Iustice still with due regard,
Respect no person nor reward.

The Prouerbe saith, a man must neuer passe
Nor peize his ballance with vnequall weights,
As once in Rome a happie custome was,
Where equitie maintained without sleights,
And iustice was the Monarks looking glasse,
Till auarice possessed their conceits:
    Then ciuill discord set their hearts at warre,
    And caused each man his owne good to marre.

EMBLEME XI.

Try well thy friend before thou trust,
Lest he do leaue thee in the dust.

Ioin hands with none, nor make of him thy frend
Whom first thou hast not proued well and tryde,
His faith may fleete and faile thee in the end,
Whose bad conditions were not first descryde;
Know well his life and maners, ere thou lend
Or giue him trust, if trust in him abide:
   For he that makes a friend of euery stranger,
   Discards him not againe without some danger.
                              No-

Nothing can temper young mens rage
Till they be tamed with old age.

Youth is too hote, and voyd of care and dread;
The aged cold, and full of doubt and feares:
Youth casts no dangers in his hastie head,
Where age with foresight warily forbeares.
Youth into needlesse quarrels soone is led,
Till oft the markes of his owne rod he weares:
　And then he learns to change the course he run,
　Whē he hath seen & known what age hath dun

Vnhappie be some that be wise,
And fooles sometime to honor rise.

In Thessalie their Asses there be kept
With special care, faire, plumpe, smooth, fat & full
Their mangers fild, their stables cleanly swept,
Though they be grosse, & thogh their pace be dul
So many times sots haue to honor leapt,
When wiser men haue had a colder pull.

  If Asses haue such lucke, what should I say?
    Let scholers burn their books, and go to play.

In friends this difference sole is tryde,
True friends stand fast, the fayned slyde.

False faith is ouer-paisd with smallest weight,
The ballance yeelds vnto the lightest fether:
The fained guest will quickly change conceit,
And in a trice will hither turne and thether;
But the sound friend will neuer sound retreit,
Nor stoope his sailes for any force of weather,
   But constantly his friendship still doth last,
   And shine the clearer in the bitter blast.

He that in finenesse would excell,
Oft marres the worke before was well.

The Painter that with curious hand and eye,
Is ouer-mending euery little line,
With too much cunning bringeth all awrye,
And marres the work that was before more fine:
So some there be thinking to soare so high,
With piercing in search of things most diuine,
  That fall so far from knowing that they sought,
  They do not know theselues so as they ought.

Search

EMBLEME XII.

Search for strange monsters farre or wide,
None like the woman wants her guide.

Great monsters mentioned are in stories found,
As was *Chymera* of a shape most wondrous,
Girion, Python, Cerb'rus that hel-hound,
Hydra, Medusa, with their heads most hideous,
Satyres and Centaures; all these same were foun'
In bodies strange, deformed and prodigious:
   Yet none more maruellous in stories read,
   Then is a woman if she want a head.

They that want knowledge do despise,
The vertues honourd of the wise.

The dirtie Swine delights more in the mire,
Then in sweete balmes that are of costly price;
Some men likewise there be, that do desire,
Rather then vertue, for to follow vice.
The blockish idiots learning none require,
Or hate euen those that are by nature wise:
  And hoggish fooles at learning will repine,
  So long as puddle shall delight the swine.

With

EMBLEME XVIII.

Within this picture are displayd,
The beauties of a woman stayd.

This picture here doth liuely represent
The beauties that may best make women prowd,
First by the Tortesse at her feete is meant,
She must not gad, but learne at home to shrowd;
Her finger to her lip is vpward bent,
To signifie she should not be too lowd:
   The key doth note, she must haue care to g
   The goods her busbād doth with pain pre

No man reapes the pleasant gaine,
But with trauell and with paine.

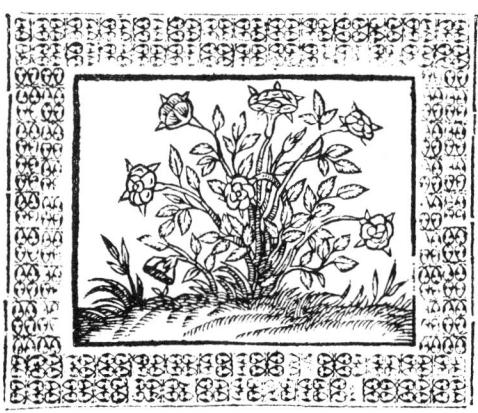

Out of the thornie and the pricking stem,
Riseth the daintie, sweetly smelling rose:
Labour and care all pleasures do inhem,
And all the wayes of profit do foreclose.
Who seeks of knowledg the most precious gem,
Must ouer-tosse full manie a wearie glose;
And through such prickles he that rose shal gain
That many seekes, and very few attaine.

They that follow fortunes guiding,
Blindly fall with often sliding.

You blinded folkes by Fortune set on hye,
Consider she is darke as well as ye,
And if your guide do want the light of eye,
You needs must fall, it can none other be.
When blind do leade the blind, they both do lye
In ditch, the Prouerbe saith, and we do see:
  And those that trust to fortunes turning wheele;
  Whé they feare least, their fall shal soonest feele.

EMBLEME XXI.

*An hypocrite is noted still,
By speaking faire and doing ill.*

Who beares a sword with honie ouer-spread,
May well be tearmed as an hypocrite,
That hides the doings of his craftie head,
With shew of sweetnesse, yeelding false delight;
Nath'lesse at last he is discouered,
When wisedome brings his subtelties to light.
   And though his sword be sharp, & cut & prick
   A little Bee shall sting him to the quicke.

A

EMBLEME XXII.

*A Prince can haue no better part,
Then Foxes wit and Lions hart.*

The Lion is of nature stout and strong,
Of courage bold, whose fiercenes none can tame
The craftie Foxe all other beasts among,
For subtill policies doth beare the name:
So to that Prince those gifts do chiefe belong,
That here on earth would purchase endlesse fame
   He like these two must frame his manners fit,
   For strength a Lion, and a Foxe for wit.

EMBLEME XXIII.

No man his mind should euer set,
To hope for that he cannot get.

Oft time when fishers plucke their nets to land,
And make great boast what fishes they shall get,
By hap a Scorpion being there at hand,
Comes vp alone inclosed in the net:
So in conceit some haue great wonders scand,
That durst presume strong Hercules to threat:
   But when they come to triall and to proofe,
   Themselues are those will stand most far aloofe.

d

EMBLEME XXIIII.

*All things out of order runne,
That are without decorum done.*

A gold ring set on snout of filthy swine,
Great weapons worne by infants yong & green
The Rogue to brag and boast him with the fi
The foolish Asse that wise himselfe doth weene;
All these to o..r vtterly repine,
And euermore .. disagree are seene.

   To keepe de.orum this good precept hold,
    Giue draffe .. swine, to tr en the rings of gold

EMBLEME XXV.

No toyle can I finde out his rest,
In euery thing the meane is best.

The bow that's drawne with ouerhardy strength,
Is found more weake then it was felt before:
By which we learne, we hurt our selues at length,
The while we labour dayly more and more:
For sloth corrupts and dulsour might & strength,
But too much toyling breeds a greater sore,
  Consuming courage so beyond all measure,
  It reaues the body of his chiefest treasure.

EMBLEME XXVI.

It is not good in peace or warre,
To presse thine enemy too farre.

Beware of quarrels with the desp'rat men,
That feare not death, nor weigh anothers life:
Good conquerors will giue place now and then
To those are vanquished in warlike strife.
And let them flie without pursuing; when
Perhaps they would else turne on them as life,
   As did the Andebats in desp'rat wise
   Run on their enemies with hoode l eyes.

EMBLEME XXVII.

hen death doth call vs at the doore,
hat ods betwixt the Prince and poore?

Eu'n as the king, the whilst we play at Chesse,
The other men in his subiection be,
Vntill the mate be giuen without redresse,
And then the king but like the rest we see;
And suffers with the little pawnes no lesse,
Then if they had no difference in degree:
    So high & low, when pleaseth death to strike,
    The Prince, the poore, are laid in graues alike.

EMBLEME XXVIII.

Fortunes blasts cannot preuaile,
To ouerthrow dame Vertues saile.

As doth the Tortesse neither feare nor feele
The idle stinging of the busie Bee;
For why his shell welnigh as hard as steele,
Keepes him as safe within as safe may be:
Eu'n so though Fortune on her wau'ring wheele
Turne vp and downe some men of high degree,
   Yet may a man with wisedome so prouide,
   To stand so sure, she sha'l not make him slide.

EMBLEME XXIX.

We see it fall out now and then,
The worser lucke the wiser men.

We see how Fortune sooner doth provide
For Robin Good-fellow and th'idle mate,
Then such as greater labours do abide,
Whose good desert she evermore doth hate.
In sleepers nets she powreth all her pride,
To painfull persons she is still vngrate:
  She hunts about to make her best profit
  For fooles & dolts, and men ẽ condi

EMBLEME XXX.

There is no sweet within our powre,
That is not sawced with some sowre.

They hurt their hand somtime that hope to gain,
And plucke the rose from off the prickling tree;
For why, no pleasure is without some paine,
The good and bad together mingled bee:
Faire weather waxeth sometime foule againe,
And after foule, faire weather oft we see.
  Wise men may note by gath'ring of this flowre,
  None reaps the sweet but he must tast the soure

EMBLEME XXXI.

Men should beware and take great heed,
To hazard friends without great need.

Who strikes the anuill rudely with his blade,
May hap to breake it with too little heed:
So he that vseth as a common trade,
To presse his friend with too too much indeed,
May chance to find his curt'sie then to fade,
When of the same he stands in greatest need.

   Thus much this Emblem in effect pretends,
   That ouerboldnesse makes leese our frends.

EMBLEME XXXII.

Great persons should not with their might,
Oppresse the poorer, though they might.

Who notes the noble bird that doth compare
All feathered fowles subiected to the skies,
And hath the Eagles princely nature found,
Which doth disdaine to litigate with flies;
Hereby may weigh and wisely vnderstand,
In base contention little honor lies:
  For he that striueth with th'inferiour sort,
  Shall with dishonor reape an ill report.

EMBLEME XXIII.

Meddle not with thy ouer-match,
Lest thou thereby most hurt do catch.

He that with razor thinks to cut the flint,
Doth vndertake a foolish fruitlesse paine,
The tender edge making but little dint,
Is soone rebated with the rockie graine,
With mightie men twere better strife to stint,
Than an vnequall quarrell to maintaine:
   Lest, as you see the razor with the stone,
    The hurt fall all to you, and they haue none.

EMBLEME XXXIIII.

Some that in knowledge diue most deepe,
Know least from hurt themselues to keepe.

The Nightingale hath such a daintie note,
No other bird the harmonie can mend;
Sometimes to sing she straineth so her throate,
That therewithall her song and life doth end:
Eu'n so likewise some students do so dote,
When others do their prose and verse commend,
   That to attaine vnto more perfect skill,
   With studying too hard themselues they kill.

EMBLEME XXXV.

The way to pleasure is so plaine,
To tread the path few can refraine.

A labyrinth is framed with such art,
The outmost entrance is both plaine and wide:
But being entred, you shall find each part,
With such odde crooked turnes on euery side,
And blind by-wayes, you shall not for your hart
Come out againe without a perfect guide:
   So to vaine pleasures it is ease to go,
   But to returne againe it is not so.

EMBLEME XXXVI.

Its hard to change an old abuse,
Wherein the heart hath taken vse.

VVho thinks to change abuses waxen old,
Is foule deceiued in his inward mind:
For they do rather grow more manifold,
And still ingender and increase their kind.
It were a foolish thing to heare it told,
That in a net a man had caught the wind:
  For thats impossible to bring to passe,
  And so is this, both now and euer was.

EMBLEME XXXVII.

Herein the chiefest cause is taught,
For which the glasses first were wrought.

A woman should, and may well without pride,
Looke in a looking-glasse, and if she find
That she is faire, then must she so prouide
To sute that beautie with so faire a mind;
If she be blacke, then that default to hide
With inward beautie of another kind.
If women would do so, they were but asses
  should dislike the vse of looking-glasses.

EMBLEME XXXVIII.

Patience brings the mind to rest,
And helps all troubles to digest.

The bird in cage restraind from libertie,
For all her bondage ceaseth not to sing;
But in the midst of all captiuitie,
With songs some cōfort she her selfe doth bring:
So when as men dŏ stand in ieopardie,
And feele that sorrowes do their sēses sting,
   Yet must they striue to put all cares away,
   And make themselues as merry as they may.

EMBLEME XXXIX.

To be a souldier good indeed,
Must of a Captaine good proceed.

Suppose a heard of Buckes should go to warre,
And by a lusty Lyon they were led:
On th'other side, if that a Bucke compare
To beare the standard as the Lyons head;
That onely Lyons force surpasseth farre, (bred:
With those he buckes, whose courage he hath
   So valiant leaders cause faint cowards fight,
     A coward Captaine mars the souldiers might.

EMBLEME XL.

Let honest truth be shield and guard,
For hanging is the theeues reward.

When as strong theeues get offices in hand,
And care not what by wrong they scrape and pull
The King doth winke, and will not vnderstand:
But when he sees that they do once waxe full,
He is content their dealing shall be scand,
And their authoritie to disanull.

  When swelling sponge is crusht, it doth restore
And yeeld the liquor it had drawne before.

EMBLEME XLI.

From one t'another taunts do go,
As doth a ball toft too and fro.

The ball flies backe to him that firſt did ſtrike,
In as great haſt, with like great force of arme:
So words for words, and blowes for blowes alike
Men ſhall receiue, wher they bring good or harm
As merchants rich great welth that ſcrape & pike
Whereby they ſit at eaſe and lye full warme,
   Giue ownce for ownce and like for like again:
   So for e ocke another ſtill we gaine.

EMBLEME XLII.

Simplicitie is of small price,
And eu'n reputed for a vice.

In Princes courts we see it so fals out,
The mildest persons are of least account,
Such as be proud, are cald braue men and stout,
Whose lofty lookes do other men surmount;
They that can cog and foist with all the rout,
Are still in prise, and do most praise amount:
   The simple man is like (as in these shapes)
   A silly Asse, amongst a sort of Ap

EMBLEME XLIII.

*When one meane failes, then by and by
Another meane we ought to try.*

When winds do ſtiſly beate againſt the ſaile,
Yet Galleys may by the maine force of ore,
So much againſt the ſpite of winds preuaile,
To come with ſafetie to the merrie ſhore:
What if one meane or purpoſe hap to faile,
Is that a reaſon we ſhould trie no more? (good,
   This will not ſerue, what though? that may be
  Is there no way but one vnto the wood?

EMBLEME XLIIII.

When warres and troubles most molest,
The wicked persons prosper best.

To fish for Eeles, they say that haue the skill,
Best be the troubled waters and the muddie:
So they that take delight in doing ill,
To trouble first the state is all their studie;
Then can they best compasse their wicked will,
And get most profit when the times be bloudie:
  Iustice in force, peaceable times and quiet
  Fits not their fishing, nor can serue their diet.

EMBLEME XLV.

Beware of fayned flattering sloes,
For none are worse then friendly foes.

False flatterers are worse than greedie crowes,
Crowes onely feed on things that we reiect,
The flatterers do oft deuower those
That are aliue, when least they do suspect;
And when they make their fairest glosing shoes,
And seeme most soundly friendship to affect,
 Then suddenly, and ere a man is ware,
 He is beguil'd and falleth in their snare.

Tho

The learned liue but poore and bare,
When fooles be rich, and better fare.

Who giues an asse the bone, a dog the hay,
May well be thought an vnwise man I trow:
Yet such disorder waxeth now a day,
Men care not how their gifts they do bestow:
Fooles are set vp in offices most gay,
The wiser men come downe and sit below.
   And now affection reason so doth smother,
   Men giue to one what doth belong t'another.

The child proct   rceuis in his
That is not chastisd in his youth.

The Ape embracing of her young one hard,
Sometimes doth kill it with her being kind,
So many parents haue their children mard,
When with fond loue and with affection blind,
They cannot chastise them with due regard,
That in their childhood be not well inclin'd.
  For when they be growne vp to state of men
  They are past mending and correcting then

EMBLEME XLVIII.

Disguised things may seeme most strange,
But nature seeld is seene to change.

Bacchus cannot himselfe so well disguise,
By clapping on his backe a Lyons skin,
But that his flagon and his bowle descries,
It is no *Hercules* that is within:
So though a foole haue shew of being wise,
By hoarie head, or by a bearded chin,
   Yet by his talke a man may quickly know,
    Whether he be discreet indeed or no.

EMBLEME XLIX.

The rich men sinne and feare no lawes,
When poore are punisht for light cause.

The Spider with her web of rare inuention,
Lies close in waite to catch the silly flies;
But with the wasp she dares not moue contentiō,
Whose force the weakenesse of her web vnties:
So rich men now against all good intentiō, (lies,
Withstād good laws, whose weight on poore mē
  And like the wasp that rends the web in sūder,
  They rule those laws that meaner mē are vnder.

EMBLEME L.

Malicious fooles worke most disgrace,
When they are set in highest place.

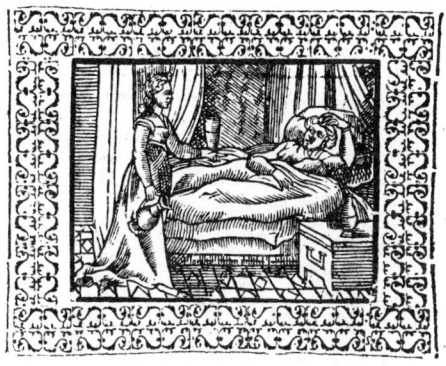

Who giues him wine a feauer doth possesse,
Augmenteth more the patients present griefe:
Wine causeth heate, the feauer doth no lesse,
Which needs must yeeld the sick but small reliefe:
Eu'n so that Prince doth little skill professe,
That a foole aloft in office chiefe,
   W   his malice he may best reueale,
   A   most hurt vnto the common weale.

EMBLEME LI.

After youth in trauell spent,
Let age be with her home content.

The painfull Pilgrime in his later dayes,
Without his leaning staffe that cannot stand,
Forsaking wife and children goes his wayes,
To seeke old relicks in a new found land;
Accounting it worth most especiall praise,
To tell what iourneyes he hath tane in han
   When he shold cut those wings if he di well,
   And like the Tortesse keepe him in his

EMBLEME L.

Malicious fooles worke most disgrace,
When they are set in highest place.

Who giues him wine a feauer doth possesse,
Augmenteth more the patients present griefe:
Wine causeth heate, the feauer doth no lesse,
Which needs must yeeld the sick but small reliefe:
Eu'n ᵢₛ that Prince doth little skill professe,
That   a foole aloft in office chiefe,
   W   his malice he may best reueale,
   A   most hurt vnto the common weale.

EMBLEME LI.

After youth in trauell spent,
Let age be with her home content.

The painfull Pilgrime in his later dayes,
Without his leaning staffe that cannot stand,
Forsaking wife and children goes his wayes,
To seeke old relicks in a new found land;
Accounting it worth most especiall praise,
To tell what iourneyes he hath tane in hand
  When he shold cut those wings if he did well,
  And like the Tortesse keepe him in his

IMPRESE.

With diligence we ought to wayt,
To flie the snares of false deceyt.

The Eagle then laments her death too late,
When as the shaft hath pierced through her brest
Who was selfe cause of such vnluckie fate,
By means the stem with her own quill was drest.
Some men to ill are so predestinate,
That though no hurt by others is profest,
   They wrong theselues by lack of taking heed,
   And are chiefe cause of their owne euill speed.

EMBLEME 4.

The liues of Princes lewdly led,
About the world are soonest spred.

Each little spot appeares more in the face,
Than any blemish in the corps beside,
The face is plainly seene in euery place,
When clothes the carkasse secretly do hide:
By which we note, that in a Princes grace,
A fault seemes greater and is sooner spide,
　　Than in some man of base and low degree,
　　As in fine cloth the brightest staines w

EMBLEME LIIII.

The Prince that would beware of harme,
Must stop his eares to flatterers charme.

When the wise birder meaneth to intrap
The foolish birds within his crafty traine,
That he may get more of them at a clap,
With prettie pipe his voice he learnes to faine:
So flatterers do not display the map
Of all their drifts in termes and speeches plaine,
  But with sweet words they couer their deceit,
  Lest Princes should perceiue & flie their bait.

E

Wit can do with little paine,
That strength alone cannot attaine.

A man by force and strength cannot attaine,
That which by stayd discretion soone is wonne,
He that doth pull the taile with might and main,
For all his force hath not so quickly done;
The other haire by haire with little paine,
In lesser time a better threed hath sponne:
  Lo here the ods betweene the wise man, pawse,
  And hastinesse of foolish furious dawes.

More

EMBLEME LVI.

More dye with surfet at their boord,
Then in the warres with dint of sword.

The glut'nous Rau'n deuours the venomd Snake
Which though at first seemes pleasant to his taft,
When he doth feele his gorge with poyson ake,
He rues with death the meate he eat in haft;
Hereby we note what heed we ought to take,
Lest that we vse excesse in our repaft:

  For gluttony doth more their deaths affoord,
  Then mighty *Mars* with his two edged sword:

E 2

EMBLEME LVII.

He that is prowdest of good hap,
Sorrow fals soonest in his lap.

Iupiter, as the learned Homer writes,
Mingleth the good and bad in such a sort,
That men obtaine not pleasures and delights,
Without some paine to waite vpon the sport;
No man with labour wearieth so his sprights,
But of some ease withall he may report:
    Nor no man yet hath euer bene so glad,
    But he hath had a time to be as sad.

Vaine

EMBLEME LVIII.

Vaine hope doth oft a man allure,
A needlesse bondage to endure.

Who so to bondage will himselfe submit,
And yet hath libertie to liue at will,
Is like a Lyon when he doth permit
A simple man with threed to hold him still;
Some are such fooles that while in court they sit,
And wast their time and all their riches spill,
   Yet will they sta   ugh they do not need,
   And not   they may break the threed

EMBLEME LIX.

He that to thrift his mind would frame,
Must not delight to follow game.

It is no time to sit still then at play,
When as the house doth burne about our eares:
Who were in flames and would not run away,
Were wondrous stout, or very void of feares;
But wisedome bids vs shorten long delay,
And to preuent the cause of future teares:
   Sith if too farre we suffer danger rome.
   Tis long againe ere t͡ be ou me.

EMBLEME LX.

A man of courage and of spright,
No foolish threatnings can affright.

Who thinks to feare the Lyon with a maske,
May proue conclusions, but preuaile no whit:
For why his force a stouter strength doth aske,
Ere that his courage can be quaild with it;
So some we see do set their tongues to taske,
And with great words that run beyond their wit
    They thinke to conquer hardie men and stout
    That of vaine brags do neither dread nor dout

EMBLEME LXI.

The man whose conscience is vnpure,
In his owne mind he is not sure.

The wicked man whose faults are manifest,
Seemes like the Hare still full of feare & dread,
He dares not sleepe nor take his quiet rest,
For doubt before some Iustice to be led;
The honest life who leades is better blest,
He euermore secure may keepe his bed,
  The while the wicked study and deuise,
  Like fearefull Hares to sleepe v̅ ͻpen eyes.

EMBLEME LXII.

Where Cupid lift to play the knaue,
He makes the Affe to brag and braue.

When Cupids ftroke tickles the inward vaines,
Oh what a power he hath to change the mind!
He makes the niggard careleffe of his gaines,
The clowne a Courtier, and the currifh kind:
Briefly his wondrous graces where he raignes,
In *Cymon* out of *Boccas* you may find;
   The little lad his Lute can finger fo,
    Would make an Affe to turne vpon the toe.

EMBLEME LXIII.

It is a point of no small cunning,
To catch Occasion at her comming.

Behold Occasion drawne before your eies,
As though she still were fleeting on her wayes,
Which image so *Lisippus* did deuise,
With knife in hand to cut off long delayes:
Her locks before bids hold ere that she flies,
Her wings do shew she can abide no stayes:
   And by her bald she tels vs at the last,
   There is no hold behind when she's past.

EMBLEME LXIIII.

The praise of beautie is but small,
Where vertue is not wynd withall.

By mens proportions we can hardly guesse,
Or know precisely whether they haue wit:
For who can tell what graces they possesse,
Although their members out of order sit:
Some heads are great, and some againe be lesse
That to their bodies do not aptly fit:
    Yet not proportion nor the bodies stature,
    But education setteth foorth the nature.

EMBLEME LXV.

*The fairest shape of th'outward part,
Shewes not the vertues of the hart.*

The stately Cypresse in his outward show,
Is straight and tall, in colour fresh and greene,
Yet on the same no wholesome fruit doth grow,
Or that to serue for nourishment is seene;
In such bare titles many men do flow,
That in their liues but barren still haue beene:
Who in experience well may some to sute,
The Cypres tree that yeelds no holsom frute

EMBLEME LXVI.

Annoint the Lawyer in his fist,
And he shall pleade eu'n what you list.

Some Lawyers waxe so deafe they cannot heare,
Or at the least they cannot vnderstand,
Except your money do so plaine appeare,
That palpably they feele it in their hand,
Giue right or wrong, your case they say is cleare,
As you would haue it, so it shall be scand:
  When double fees do walke, and money flies,
  A man would think their hands were ful of eies

EMBLEME LXVII.

Let fire or sword their choller wreake,
A constant heart can nothing breake.

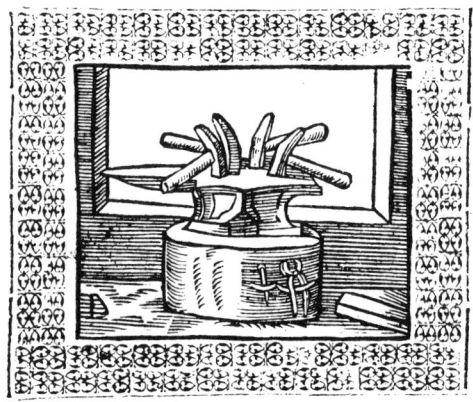

Like to the Stith I count the constant hart,
The Stith endures the heauie hammers beat,
And doth not shrinke nor yeeld in any part,
Though smiths lay on & thump it till they sweat:
Eu'n so should men in chances ouerthwart,
When pains increase & fortune seemes to threat,
   Yet in their course with constant purpose run,
   And still persist till they haue honour wonne.

EMBLEME LXVIII.

When youth is in his flowring prime,
He cares not how he passe his time.

Redeeme the time, time dearer is then gold,
And time once gone can neuer be reclaimed,
He need begin betimes that would be old,
If time be lost, our life is likewise maimed;
Yet greene young heads disdaining to be told,
As though more priuiledge of yeres they claimed
   Do seem to pull the weight with al their sway,
   And wast their time, and hast their dying day.

EMBLEME LXIX.

He that himselfe is voide of wit,
In a wise man despiseth it.

Some say the Camell will not stoope to drinke,
Till he hath first defil'd it with his feete:
So in our time rude people vse to thinke,
That perfect eloquence is most vnmeete:
In whose dull heads this reason will not sinke,
That eloquence should proue a thing so sweete:
 Such is their folly, and their sense so blind,
 They count this gift but of the basest kind.

Greedie

EMBLEME LXX.

Greedy gaping after gaine,
Will make a man take any paine.

The hope for gaine, and thirst for worldly goods
Compels a man to venture rocks and seas,
Neither can waters deepe nor raging floods,
Cause any kind of perils to displease;
Men scrape out goods out of the myrie muds,
For lucres sake all labours seeme but ease:
  And to prouide themselues of things they lacke
  There be wil swim with burdens on their backe.

EMBLEME LXXI.

There is no thing can be more deere,
Than Time, if we could keepe it heere.

The fleeting Time doth quickly steale away,
Which once let passe, returneth not againe,
Therefore tis good to take Time while we may,
Lest afterward we rue our losse in vaine:
Time tarrieth none, the Prouerbe old doth say,
Then vse it well the while it doth remaine:
   For those that leade their liues in belly-cheare,
   Do leese their time, of al things else most deare

EMBLEME LXXII.

In time all things shall be revealed,
That are most secretly concealed.

Greene fruits and floures do ripen by the Sunne,
Whose raies bring forth their beauties and their
Eu'n so whē youth with time is ouer-run, (smel:
Though it were greene, and though it often fell,
Yet riper yeares will mend all errors done,
And make men liue more vertuously and well:
And time doth change and alter mens behauior
As by the Sunne the flowers mend their sauor.

F 2

EMBLEME LXXIII.

A traytor and a flattering friend,
Say that they neuer do intend.

The flatterers and traytors both be such,
That with their words their thoghts do not agree
For till iust triall bring them to the tuch,
They seeme in shew most faithfull friends to bee:
But little will they do professing much,
And inwardly from friendship they do flee:
    Who when their hart behind they do conuay,
    They beare in hand their tongue another way

EMBLEME LXXIIII.

With some light thing when thou needs must,
Try thou thy friend before thou trust.

We proue at first if that a pot will hold,
With water, not with wine of any kind,
To th'end the losse the lesse we may behold,
If in the bottome any hole we find;
So ere to trust a stranger ye waxe bold,
Tell him the lightest secret of your mind,
  Whereof small danger growes another day,
  If he the same your secret should bewray.

EMBLEME LXXV.

Reason bids vs haue a care,
That others harmes make vs beware.

In Affrica if Lyons hanged there,
Do terrifie the rest that them behold,
Why do not theeues and robbers likewise feare,
That still commit most wicked acts for gold?
And Magistrates that such great office beare,
By like examples feare to be too bold:
   For they may know, except they do amend,
   By such lewd liuing they may haue like end.

ABLEME LXXVI.

We purchase nothing by our play,
But beggery and our decay.

They that do vse to hazard much at play,
And venter all their substance at a cast,
Do often fall into so great decay,
That they become meere beggers at the last:
And then of others they are faine to pray,
Or liue of spoile, and others goods to wast:
   When as their owne before with better thrift,
   Would wel haue seru'd their turn at eu'ry shift.

EMBLEME LXXVII

All those that Loue do fancy most,
But leeje their labour and their cost.

Fond Loue is chiefly likened to a flue,
In which the more you poure the water in,
The more is spilt, by letting thorow driue,
And you no neare then when you first begin:
Eu'n so for loue when young men frankly giue,
Till oft they leaue themselues not worth a pin:
    When all is spent, and they liue by the losse,
    They turne againe at last by weeping crosse.

EMBLEME LXXVIII.

*A woman is of such a kind,
That nothing can content her mind.*

Who so a ship would vndertake to store,
And furnish her with all that she doth lacke,
He needs to haue his purse well lyn'd before,
And shall find worke enough to hold him tacke:
Yet women are as chargeable or more,
Who still are wanting one or other knacke:
  So that who would be busi'd all his life,
  May best be troubled with a ship or wife.

EMBLEME LXXIX.

A thousand dangers dayly grow
Of foolish Loue, as louers know.

Alas that men should follow Venus trace,
And take delight to play on Cupids bits,
Who casteth downe from high estate to base,
And makes men counted wise, to leese their wits;
None but vnhappie wretches voyd of grace,
Do euer fall into such franticke fits:
  Vpon repentance fire he puts the Still (distill.
  And blowes the coles, where nought t teares

EMBLEME LXXX.

The fruite of loue is very strange,
It hath so many kinds of change.

The fruits of Loue are diuers in effect,
Some good, some bad, some witherd, some are (greene,
Some sweet, som soure, som wholsom, som infect,
And some are secret, some are plainly seene:
Now in regard, to morrow quite reiect,
Oft in prosperitie, and then in teene:
   They change as often, and do alter soone,
   Eu'n as vnconstant as we see the Moone.

EMBLEME LXXXI.

In all his stocks blind Loue doth set
The graffes of griefe our hearts to fret.

If any man a perfect Gardiner lacks,
Here shall he find one of no common skill,
For sundry graffes, for knots and pretty knacks,
He neuer will be idle by his will.
What euer he doth set or sow, will waxe,
And all your stocks with some plants he will fill,
  But with the rest he graffeth alwaies chiefe,
  The choaking peare of anguish and of griefe.

EMBLEME LXXXII.

Ungratefull men breed great offence,
As persons voyd of wit or sence.

The Oke doth suffer the yong Yuy wind
Vp by his sides, till it be got on hy,
But being got aloft it so doth bind,
It kils the stocke that it was raised by:
So some proue so vnthankfull and vnkind,
To those on whom they chiefly do rely,
    By whom they first were called to their state,
    They be the first (I say) giue them the mate.

EMBLEME LXXXIII.

It is a point of great foresight,
Into your selues to looke aright.

We reade how in Phœnicia long ago,
The people rais'd this figure vp on hie,
Where as the same might make the fairest shoe,
And men obserue what it did signifie.
The Serpent in a circle painted so,
Thus much doth teach to vnderstand thereby,
 That in the world there is no greater thing,
 Then man to know himselfe in euery thing.

EMBLEM XXIIII.

On others some presume to prey,
And fall themselues into decay.

The Faulcon sometime greedie of her pray,
Finds her owne foote fast tide vnto the tree,
So are there some lay waite on others way,
That are themselues the first that harmed bee:
Who digs a pit for other mens decay,
Ma ll therein himselfe we often see,
     feel the plagues i is own person then
      h he ordain'd t nish other men

EMBLEM LXXXV.

Who labours that to bring to passe
That cannot be, is but an Asse.

The cannon charg'd with lesse then doth behoue,
The heauy bullet farre off cannot throw:
And none hath seene the weighty windmil moue
If one but with a payre of bellowes blow:
This shewes we should in euery action proue,
With due proportion how each thing should goe;
　As wise men neuer will attempt the thing,
　That first they know to passe they cannot bring

EMBLEME LXXXVI.

The Prelates life should shine as cleare,
As lampe on mountaine doth appeare.

The Prelates vertues ought to shine so bright,
As doth a lampe set on a mountaine hie,
From whose good deeds should issue such a light
That other men might see and walke thereby:
Through his example when it is not right,
The silly people oft do walke awry; (stands
  And then the Lord whose vēgeance none with
  The bloud of those requireth at his hands.

In euery thing aduise you furst:
Take the best, and leaue the wurst.

n Poets pamphlets fables fond we find,
Yet in those fables wisedome they inuent,
The morall still hath sense of other kind,
How ere the verse do colour their intent:
But to the letter who himselfe doth bind,
May misse the matter that therein is ment:
  As vnder leaues that hang on crooked vines,
  Lie hid sweet grapes that make the costly wines

EMBLEME LXXXVII.

No surety in a womans mind,
Her fancie changeth with the wynd.

A womans constancie is euen as sure,
As if one held an Eele fast by the taile,
Her faith nor loue do neuer long endure,
But fleete away as sunne doth melt the haile:
As many authors, Greeke and Latine pure,
Haue left in writing for our more auaile,
   That womens words mens eares do so delight,
   They make them oft beleeue the crow is white

EMBLEME LXXXIX.

No shade of enuy can obscure
The light of vertue shining pure.

When as the Sunne stands iust aboue the head,
The bodie shewes but short and slender shade;
Eu'n so whē vertue her bright beams doth spred,
The smoke of enuie soone away doth fade:
Vertue doth make men liue when they be dead,
Though enuy brag, & thogh she draw her blade,
   In spite thereof yet vertuous men shall gaine
   Honour and praise, for euer to remaine.

EMBLEME XC.

A word once spoken though in vaine,
It cannot be recald againe.

It is too late to catch the bird againe,
That once hath bid her keepers hands adue:
So when a man lets slip a word in vaine,
His speech once past is not recald anew;
For words will fly from mouth to mouth amaine
Whereof great quarrels oftentimes ensue:

   Therefore be wise, and in your speech preuēt
   To speak such words as you may chance repēt

EMBLEME XCI.

None waxe more proud we lightly see,
Then beggers rais'd to high degree.

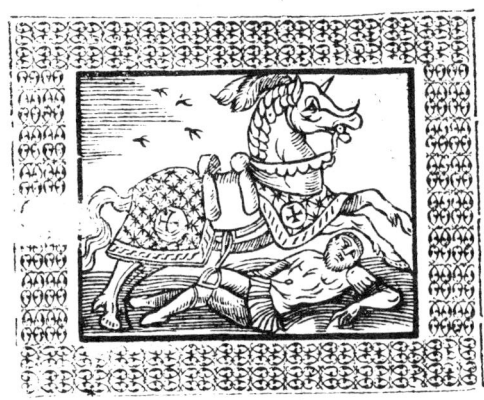

Bucephalus was then in chiefest pride,
When he had felt rich armour on his backe,
And onely *Alexander* him might ride,
When no man else could hold him any tacke.
Hereby we note a thing that oft is trine,
How such as are but base and in great lacke,
   When to new honor by good hap they grow,
   Their old acquaintance they disdain to know.

EMBLEME XCII.

Loue and feare are chiefest things,
That stablish Scepters vnto kings.

A Prince that would his fame should stil increase
And honour to resound in euery place,
He shall assure his Scepter with more ease,
If that his subiects loue and feare his face.
A Dog and Hare two enemies to peace,
One loues, the other feareth in like case:
   Yet better peace to Princes neuer springs,
   Then when like Dogs & Hares men serue

EMBLEME XCI.

He that would leade a happie life,
For vertue let him chufe his wife.

Some do not care how nor with who they linke,
If fading beautie pleafe their wanton eye,
Others fo they be fingring of the chinke,
Care not how foone their hand be in the pie,
But a wife man doth warily forethinke,
That both thofe courfes run too farre awrie,
 That this nor that, is neither here nor there,
 The chiefeft choife is chufing by the eare.

No kind of friend will longer stay,
When riches once are gone away.

The lyce do shun the place where they were bred
When life to leaue the carkasse they do find:
So when mens fortune failes and waxeth dead,
And when their wealth and riches do vnwind,
We see the flatterers away are fled
From those to whom the same were earst inclin
   This shewes, that in aduersitie and need,
   Tis hard to find a trustie friend indeed.

EMBLEME XCV.

When thou for ayd to God doſt pray,
To helpe thy ſelfe thou muſt aſſay.

When thou ſhalt trauell on the tedious way,
Aud ſee thy Aſſe fall loden in the mire,
Firſt for the helpe of God prepare to pray,
That ſuccours all that do his helpe require;
But in the meane time ceaſe not to aſſay,
 With thy own hands to draw him from the mire:
  For he that would the helpe of God attaine,
   To helpe himſelfe muſt take ſome litle paine.

A wanton woman and a light,
Will not be tam'd by art nor might.

With greater ease the Dolphin is restrained,
Then wanton women bridled of their will,
Who from their purpose cannot be constrained,
They are so full of craft and subtill skill: (ned,
Wel may they boast what guerdon they haue gai-
Than can subiect their wiues vnto their will;
   For oft the ayer of a womans smocke
   Withstands alone the bonds of chast wedlock.

Constancie hath most renowne,
When crosses most do beare vs downe.

The more that Saffron troden is with feete,
The more it still doth flourish on the ground:
So when with troubles vertuous minds do meet,
The more oppreft, the ftronger they be found:
Where vertue is, there may we plainest fee't,
In those whom cares & woes do cōpasse round:
   And when aduersitie doth most assaile,
    By striuing then aloft to beare their saile.

EMBLEME XCVIII.

Who so to studie doth incline,
The hardest wit it shall refine.

Though childrens wit be not so ripe and quicke,
As vnto others nature doth impart,
Paine will help out where nature seemes to stick,
And they great maisters made of many an Art;
Eu'n as the Beare doth into fashion licke
The lumpe she laid without proportiond part;
  For man is made againe by reasons helpe,
  As is new moulded the mis-shapen whelpe.

EMBLEME XCIX.

*When some thinke most themselues in peace,
Their dangers oft do most increase.*

When Hercles had ordaind to take his rest,
And from his former labours him withdrew,
Hydra that monstrous seuen-headed beast
Against him came, his troubles to renew.
Eu'n so when vertue hath her hire possest,
And once attained vnto honor due,
  Some chance or other by fowle enuy growes,
  And still new troubles and new trauels sowes.

THE THEATER OF FINE DEVICES,

containing an hundred morall Emblemes.

First penned in French by Guillaume de la Perriere, *and translated into English by*
THOMAS COMBE.

LONDON,
Printed by Richard Field.
1614.

TO THE HIGH
AND MIGHTY PRINCESSE,
Ladie Marguerite of France, Queene of
Nauarre, and the onely sister of the most
Christian King of France.

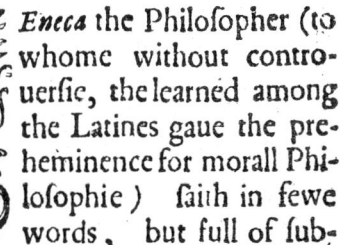
Eneca the Philosopher (to whome without controuersie, the learned among the Latines gaue the preheminence for morall Philosophie) saith in fewe words, but full of substance, that Fortune is neuer at rest; and further, that she vseth not to giue ioy without sadnesse, sweete without sowre, rest without labour, honour without enuie, and generally no felicitie vvithout his contrary: the vvhich novv I perceiue to be verified in my selfe. For vvhereas shee hath giuen me occasion of ioy

A 3

The Epistle Dedicatory.

in offering mee an oportunity to shew my dutifull reuerence to your royall Maiestie, and also to our famous Citie, by your happy approach thither: thereby she hath made me sad and melancholious, in that she hath so much hastened your said coming, that I had not the leisure to prepare and file these hundred morall Emblemes, accompanied with an hundred staues of verses, expositors of the same: the which in their first inuention (such as they are) I dedicate to your most excellent Maiestie. But that your Maiestie may not blame me, in that (following the errour of the Gentiles and Ethnickes) I attribute to Fortune that which (as a Christian writing to a Christian Princesse) I ought to attribute to Gods prouidence: I say therefore, that your said happy comming depēded not any whit vpon fortune, but (euen as do all other humane actions) onely vpon Gods prouidence, who (as it is necessary to beleeue) doth all things for the best: and that consequently your sayd coming hath not bene to me hastie, but for the best. Wherefore considering

The Epistle Dedicatorie.

sidering the precedent with my selfe, I do presume humbly to present vnto your Maiestie my said Emblemes, although they haue attained but to halfe the number that I intended; beseeching your Maiestie to receiue them (such as they are) according to your accustomed benignitie, and that with so good a will as they are by me your poore seruant offered and presented. Moreouer (Madame) it is not onely in our time that Emblemes are in account and singular regard, but it hath bene of ancient times and almost from the beginning of the world: for the Egyptians (which thinke themselues to be the the first people of the world) before the vse of letters, wrote by figures & images, as well of men, beasts, fowles, and fishes, as of serpents, thereby expressing their intentions, as is written by most ancient authors, *Chæremon*, *Orus*, *Apollo*, and the like, which haue laboured diligently and curiously to expound the saide hieroglyphicall figures: whereof likewise *Lucan* maketh mention in his *Pharsalie*, and *Polyphile* the author of the

The Epistle Dedicatorie.

Moderns, in the description of his dreame, *Clius Rhodiginus* in his commentaries of the ancient readings. *Alciat* hath likewise in our time set out certaine Emblemes, and adorned them with Latine verses. And I (imitating these abouesaid) esteem the time wel bestowed, which I employed in the deuising & beautifying of these saide Emblemes: and I shall think my selfe most happy, if the reading herof may yeeld you any honest recreation: praying God (most noble Princesse) that he will send you long life and euerlasting happinesse.

Your humble seruant,
Guillaume de la Perriere.

To the Reader.

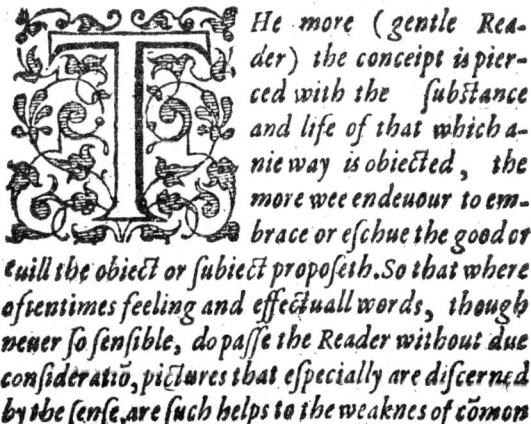

He more (gentle Reader) the conceipt is pierced with the substance and life of that which anie way is obiected, the more wee endeuour to embrace or eschue the good or euill the obiect or subiect proposeth. So that where oftentimes feeling and effectuall words, though neuer so sensible, do passe the Reader without due consideratiō, pictures that especially are discerned by the sense, are such helps to the weaknes of cōmon vnderstandings, that they make words as it were

To the Reader.

deedes, and set the whole substance of that which is offered, before the sight and conceict of the Reader. Therefore for instruction sake is his labour worthilie bestowed, that vndertooke and accomplished the Translation of this booke: contayning precepts and rebukes to our behauiours.

wherein if the verse be any thing obscure, the Impreses or pictures make it more liuely, and in a manner actuall. For the credite and acceptation of it, let the estimation which it had in the French suffise to grace and commend it Englished: being dedicated vnto the Queene of Nauarre, whose dignity should not haue bene presented with a worke of any small value. which suppositions and authorities though they make it nothing the better, yet serue they verie worth·ly to moue thy desire to the triall of the Contents, both by seeing and reading them. wherein let not the common conceipts of the world withdrawe thy minde, which hateth any thing that is bitter, to their flattering delightes: but mooued with thine owne profite, and

To the Reader.

and helpe of thy better part, requite the Translatours paines in reading and obseruing, and thou shalt double his deserts in thine owne profite.

EMBLEME I.

According to the time forepast,
Be wisely warned at the last.

Ianus is figur'd with a double face,
To note at once the time to come and past.
So should the wise obserue the passed space,
As they may well foresee a chance at last,
And with such prouidence direct this race,
That in their thoughts both times be euer plaste:
  Embracing vertue then in euery thing,
  Themselues to rest and quiet peace shall bring
                                                Ven'ry

EMBLEME II.

*Ven'rie and drinke do now and then
Besot some of the wisest men.*

We reade when *Bacchus* faire dame *Venus* met,
They two together walked forth in chase,
Forthwith their engines and their snares they set
T'intrap the next that should come in the place:
And straight *Minerua* taken in the net,
Was holden prisoner in a wofull case.
  By which is shewne, as we may plaine perceiue
  That wine and women wisest folke deceiue.

EMBLEME III.

Who doth presume aboue his state,
Doth still incurre the greater hate.

Thou that in Court doest spend thy merry daies,
Sport not with Princes, if that thou be wise:
For he that with his owne superiour playes,
Shall finde great perils thereof to arise.
Meddle with thy match, the antiēt prouerbe saies
On equall play-fellowes no danger lyes.
   He that presumes to shaue the Lyons skin,
   Full little knowes what danger he is in.

EMBLEME IIII.

In pleasures vaine no time bestow,
Lest it procure your ouerthrow.

The Flie so often to the milke pan vseth,
That in sweete milke at last her death she taketh:
The foole delights in pleasures that he chuseth,
So long vntill his ruine he awaketh.
But happie he, who so in time refuseth,
And all vaine fancies vtterly forsaketh. (ction,
  Such one with heed, and graue & good instru-
  Doth wisely shun his perill and destruction.

EMBLEME LV.

One bird in hand is better farre,
Then three which in the hedges are.

Who doth expect the bals vncertaine bound,
And quite permit the certaine flight go by,
A player bad at tennis he is found,
And gets but seldome any good thereby.
So some neglect the true and perfect ground,
And for vaine hope do wander quite awry:
   That with fond enterprises and vaine glory,
   With diuers troubles haue thēselues made sory

Most

EMBLEME VI.

Most men do vse some colour'd shift.
For to conceal their craftie drift.

Masks will be more hereafter in requeſt,
And grow more deare than they did heretofore:
They ſeru'd then onely but in play and ieſt,
For merriment, and to no purpoſe more:
Now be they vſde in earneſt of the beſt,
And of ſuch Maſkers there abound ſuch ſtore,
   That you ſhall finde but few in any place,
   That carrie not ſometimes a double face.

B

EMBLEME VII.

He that doth loue to liue at ease,
An angry man must not displease.

Who will with sword be foding of the fire,
Must looke to haue the sparks flie in his face:
They that delight with speech as sharpe as brire
To choler others with an humour base,
Vnlooked for perhaps shall finde retire,
Wordes or else deeds, vnto their owne disgrace.
  He that will stirre the angry man thats still,
  Assure himselfe, his hands shall quickly fill.

EMBLEME VIII.

It were a foolish senslesse part,
With griefe and care to eate thy heart.

The wise *Pythagoras* hath euer taught,
Man should not eat vp his owne proper heart,
Nor as a stranger to himselfe be brought
To waste his life with sorrow and with smart;
But so himselfe to temper still he ought,
That woes and cares may vanish from each part:
  Sith nothing hinders more a mans wel-fare,
  Then lingring sorrow, heauinesse and care

EMBLEME IX.

There be some fooles the cords do spin,
Wherein themselues be netted in.

Who striues to set a narrow ring and straight
Vpon his finger, which too grosse he finds,
Like to the foole that bytes at eu'ry bayt,
Himselfe with his owne folly often binds.
While for felicity some thinke they wait,
They fall in bondages of diuerse kinds:
   But wise men vse their fortitude to shunne
   Such seruitudes as fooles into doe runne.

EMBLEME X.

Vse iustice still with due regard,
Respect no person nor reward.

The Prouerb saith, a man must neuer passe
Nor peize his ballance with vnequall weights;
As once in Rome a happie custome was,
Where equity maintained without sleights,
And iustice was the Monarks looking glasse,
Till auarice possessed their conceits:
   Then ciuill discord set their hearts at warre,
   And caused each man his owne good to marre.

EMBLEME XI.

Try well thy friend before thou trust,
Lest he do leaue thee in the dust.

Ioin hands with none, nor make of him thy friend
Whom first thou hast not proued well and tride:
His faith may fleete and faile thee in the end,
Whose bad conditions were not first descryde.
Know well his life and manners ere thou lend
Or giue him trust, if trust in him abide:
   For he that makes a friend of euery stranger,
    Discards him not againe without some danger.

EMBLEME XII.

Nothing can temper yong mens rage,
Till they be tamed with old age.

Youth is too hote, and voyd of care and dread;
The aged cold, and full of doubts and feares:
Youth casts no dangers in his hastie head,
Where age with foresight warily forbeares.
Youth into needlesse quarrels soone is led,
Till oft the markes of his owne rod he weares:
  And then he learns to change the course he run,
  Whē he hath seen & known what age hath dun.

EMBLEME XIII.

Vnhappie be some that be wise,
And fooles sometime to honor rise.

In Thessalie their Asses there be kept
With speciall care, faire, plumbe, smooth, fat & ful,
Their mangers fild, their stables cleanly swept,
Though they be grosse, & thogh their pace be dul
So many times sots haue to honour leapt,
When wiser men haue had a colder pull.
  If Asses haue such lucke, what should I say?
  Let schollers burn their books, and go to play.

EMBLEME XIIII.

In friends this difference sole is tryde,
True friends stand fast, the fained slide.

Falſe faith is ouer-peiſd with ſmalleſt weight,
The ballance yeelds vnto the lighteſt fether:
The fained gueſt will quickly change conceit,
And in a trice will hither turne and thither.
But the ſound friend will neuer ſound retreit,
Nor ſtoope his ſailes for any force of weather,
   But conſtantly his friendſhip ſtil doth laſt,
   And ſhine the clearer in the bitter blaſt.

EMBLEME XV.

He that in fineneſſe would excell,
Oft marres the worke before was well.

The Painter that with curious hand and eye,
Is ouer-mending euery little line,
With to much cunning bringeth all awrye,
And marres the worke that was before more fine.
So some there be thinking to soare so high,
With piercing in search of things most diuine,
  That fall so far from knowing that they sought,
  They do not know theſelues so as they ought.

Search

EMBLEME XVI.

*Search for strange monsters farre or wide,
None like the woman wants her guide.*

Great monsters mentioned are in stories found,
As was *Chymera* of a shape most wondrous,
Girion, Python, Cerb'rus that hel-hound,
Hydra, Medusa, with their heads most hideous,
Satyres and Centaures; all these same were found
In bodies strange, deformed and prodigious:
   Yet none more maruellous in stories read,
   Then is a woman if she want a head.

EMBLEME XVII.

They that want knowledge, do despise
The vertues honoured of the wise.

The dirty Swine delights more in the mire,
Then in sweete balmes that are of costly price.
Some men likewise there be, that do desire,
Rather then vertue for to follow vice.
The blockish idiots learning none require,
But hate euen those that are by nature wise:
    And hoggish fooles at learning will repine,
  So long as puddle shall delight the swine.

Within

EMBLEME XVIII.

Within this picture are displaid,
The beauties of a woman stayd.

This picture here doth liuely represent
The beauties that may best make women proud;
First by the Tortesse at her feete is meant,
She must not gad, but learne at home to shrowd;
Her finger to her lip is vpward bent,
To signifie she should not be too lowd:
    The key doth note, she must haue care to guide
    The goods her husbād doth with pain prouide.

EMBLEME XIX.

No man reapes the pleasant graine,
But with trauell and with paine.

Out of the thornie and the pricking stem,
Riseth the dainty, sweetly smelling rose:
Labour and care all pleasures do inhem,
And all the wayes of profit do foreclose.
Who seekes of knowledg the most precious gem,
Must ouer-tosse full many a wearie glose;
  And through such prickles he that rose shal gain
  That many seekes, and very few attaine,

EMBLEME XX.

They that follow fortunes guiding,
Blindly fall with often sliding.

You blinded folkes by Fortune set on hye,
Consider she is darke as well as ye,
And if your guide do want the light of eye,
You needs must fall, it can none other be.
When blind do leade the blind, they both do lye
In ditch, the Prouerbe saith, and we do see:
  And those that trust to fortunes turning wheele,
  Whē they feare least, their fall shall soonest feele.

EMBLEME XXI.

An hypocrite is noted still,
By speaking faire, and doing ill.

Who beares a sword with honie ouer-spread,
May well be tearmed as an hypocrite,
That hides the doings of his craftie head,
With shew of sweetnes yeelding false delight;
Nath'lesse at last he is discouered,
When wisedome brings his subtilties to light,
 And though his sword be sharp, & cut & prick,
 A little Bee shall sting him to the quicke.

EMBLEME XXII.

*A Prince can haue no better part,
Then Foxes wit and Lions heart.*

The Lyon is of nature ſtout and ſtrong,
Of courage bold, whoſe fierceneſs none can tame;
The craftie Foxe all other beaſts among,
For ſubtill policies doth beare the name.
So to that Prince thoſe gifts do chiefe belong,
That here on earth would purchaſe endles fame:
   He like theſe two muſt frame his manners fit,
   For ſtrength a Lion, and a Foxe for wit.

C

EMBLEME XXIII.

No man his minde should euer set,
To hope for that he cannot get.

Oft time when fishers plucke their nets to land,
And make great boast what fishes they shall get,
By hap a Scorpion being there at hand,
Comes vp alone inclosed in the net.
So in conceit some haue great wonders scand,
That durst presume strong *Hercules* to threat:
  But when they come to triall and to proofe,
  Themselues are those will stand most far aloofe.

All

EMBLEME XXIIII.

All things out of order runne,
That are without decorum *done.*

A gold ring set on snout of filthy swine,
Great weapons worne by infants yong & greene,
The Rogue to brag and boast him with the fine,
The foolish Asse that wise himselfe doth weene;
All these to order vtterly repine,
And euermore to disagree are seene.
  To keepe *decorum* this good precept hold,
  Giue draffe to swine, to men the rings of gold.

EMBLEME XXV.

No toile can laſt without his reſt,
In euery thing the meane is beſt.

The bow that's drawn with ouer hardy ſtrength,
Is found more weake then it was felt before.
By which we learne, we hurt our ſelues at length,
The while we labour dayly more and more.
For ſloth corrupts & duls our might & ſtrength;
But too much toyling breeds a greater ſore,
   Conſuming courage ſo beyond all meaſure,
   It reaues the body of his chiefeſt treaſure.

It

EMBLEME XXVI.

It is not good in peace or warre,
To preſſe thine enemie too farre.

Beware of quarrels with the deſp'rat men,
That feare not death, nor weigh anothers life:
Good conquerors will giue place now and then
To thoſe are vanquiſhed in warlike ſtrife,
And let them flie without purſuing; when
Perhaps they would elſe turne on them as rife.
   As did the Andebats in deſp'rat wiſe
   Run on their enemies with hooded eyes.

EMBLEME XXVII.

When death doth call us at the doore,
What ods betwixt the Prince and poore?

Eu'n as the king, the whilst we play at Chesse,
The other men in his subiection be,
Vntill the mate be giuen without redresse,
And then the king but like the rest we see;
And suffers with the little pawnes no lesse,
Then if they had no difference in degree.

So high and low, when pleaseth death to strike,
The Prince, the poore, are laid in graues alike.

Fortunes

EMBLEME XXVIII.

Fortunes blasts cannot preuaile,
To ouerthrow dame Vertues saile.

As doth the Tortesse neither feare nor feele
The idle stinging of the busie Bee;
For why his shell welnigh as hard as steele,
Keepes him as safe within as safe may be:
Eu'n so though Fortune on her wan'ring wheele,
Turne vp and downe some men of high degree,
   Yet may a man with wisedome so prouide,
    To stand so sure, she shall not make him slide.

EMBLEME XXIX.

We see it fall out now and then,
The worser lucke the wiser men.

We see how Fortune sooner doth prouide
For Robin Good-fellow and th'idle mate,
Than such as greater labours do abide,
Whose good desert she euermore doth hate:
In sleepers nets she powreth all her pride,
To painfull persons she is still vngrate:
   She hunts about to make her best prouision,
   For fooles and dolts, & men of base condition.

There

EMBLEME XXX.

There is no sweet within our powre,
That is not sauced with some sowre.

They hurt their hand sometime that hope to gain,
And placke the rose from off the prickling tree;
For why, no pleasure is without some paine,
The good and bad together mingled be;
Faire weather waxeth sometime foule againe,
And after foule faire weather oft we see.

  Wise men may note by gath'ring of this flowre,
None reaps the sweet but he must tast the soure.

EMBLEME XXXI.

Men should beware and take great heed,
To hazard friends without great need.

Who strikes the anuill rudely with his blade,
May hap to breake it with too little heed:
So he that vseth as a common trade,
To presse his friend with too too much indeed,
May chance to finde his curt'sie then to fade,
When of the same he stands in greatest need.
  Thus much this Embleme in effect pretends,
  That ouer boldnes makes vs leese our friends.
Great

EMBLEME XXXII.

Great persons should not with their might,
Oppresse the poorer, though they might.

Who notes the noble bird that doth command,
All feathered fowles subiected to the skies,
And hath the Eagles princely nature scand,
Which doth disdaine to litigate with flies;
Hereby may weigh and wisely vnderstand,
In base contention little honour lies.

    For he that striueth with th'inferiour sort,
Shall with dishonour reape an ill report.

EMBLEME XXXIII.

Meddle not with thy ouer-match.
Lest thou thereby most hurt do catch.

He that with razor thinks to cut the flint,
Doth vndertake a foolish fruitlesse paine,
The tender edge making but little dint,
Is soone rebated with the rockie graine.
With mightie men twere better strife to stint,
Than an vnequall quarrell to maintaine:
   Lest, as you see the razor with the stone,
   The hurt fall all to you, and they haue none.

Some

EMBLEME XXXIIII.

Some that in knowledge diue most deepe,
Know least from hurt themselues to keepe.

The Nightingale hath such a daintie note,
No other bird the harmonie can mend;
Sometimes to sing she straineth so her throte,
That therewithall her song and life doth end.
Eu'n so likewise some students do so dote,
When others do their prose and verse commend,
   That to attaine vnto more perfect skill,
   With studying too hard themselues they kill.

EMBLEME XXXV.

The way to pleasure is so plaine,
To tread the paths few can refraine.

A labyrinth is framed with such art,
The outmost entrance is both plaine and wide:
But being entred, you shall finde each part,
With such odde crooked turnes on euery side,
And blind by-waies, you shall not for your heart
Come out againe without a perfect guide.
 So to vaine pleasures it is ease to go,
 But to returne againe it is not so.

EMBLEME XXXVI.

Its hard to change an old abuse,
Wherein the heart hath taken use.

Who thinks to change abuses waxen old,
Is foule deceiued in his inward mind:
For they do rather grow more manifold,
And still ingender and increase their kind.
It were a foolish thing to heare it told,
That in a net a man hath caught the wind:
   For thats impossible to bring to passe,
   And so is this, both now and euer was.

EMBLEME XXXVII.

Herein the chiefest cause is taught,
For which the glasses first were wrought.

A woman should, and may well without pride,
Looke in a looking glasse; and if she find
That she is faire, then must she so prouide
To sute that beautie with to faire a mind.
If she be blacke, then that default to hide
With inward beautie of another kind.

If women would do so, they were but asses
That should dislike the vse of looking-glasses.
Patience

EMBLEME XXXVIII.

Patience brings the minde to rest,
And helps all troubles to digest.

The bird in cage restraind from libertie,
For all her bondage ceasseth not to sing.
But in the midst of all captiuitie,
With songs some cófort she her selfe doth bring.
So when as men do stand in ieopardie,
And feele that sorrowes do their senses sting,
    Yet must they striue to put all cares away,
    And make themselues as merry as they may.

EMBLEME XXXIX.

To be a soldier good indeed,
Must of a Captaine good proceed.

Suppose a heard of Buckes should go to warre,
And by a lusty Lyon they were led:
On th'other side, if that a Bucke compare
To beare the standard as the Lyons head;
That onely Lyons force surpasseth farre, (bred.
With those his Bucks, whose courage he hath
  So valiant leaders cause faint cowards fight,
  A coward Captaine mars the soldiers might.

Let

EMBLEME XL.

Let honest truth be shield and guard,
For hanging is the theeues reward.

When as strong theeues get offices in hand,
And care not what by wrong they scrape and pul,
The King doth winke, and will not vnderstand:
But when he sees that they do once waxe full,
He is content their dealing shall be scand,
And their authority to disanull.
  When swelling sponge is crusht, it doth restore
And yeeld the liquor it had drawne before.

EMBLEME XLI.

From one t' another taunts do go,
As doth a ball tost too and fro.

The ball flies backe to him that first did strike,
In as great haste, with like great force of arme:
So words for words, and blowes for blowes alike
Men shall receiue, wher they bring good or harm.
As merchāts rich great wealth that scrape & pike,
Whereby they sit at ease and lye full warme,
  Giue ownce for ownce, and like for like again:
  So for one mocke another still we gaine.
Simplicity

EMBLEME XLII.

*Simplicitie is of small price,
And eu'n reputed for a vice.*

In Princes courts we see it so fals out,
The mildest persons are of least account:
Such as be proud, are called braue men and stout,
Whose lofty lookes do other men surmount;
They that can cog and foist with all the rout,
Are still in prise, and do most praise amount.
   The simple man is like (as in these shapes)
   A silly Asse amongst a sort of Apes.

EMBLEME XLIII.

*When one meane failes, then by and by,
Another meane we ought to try.*

When winds do ftifly beate againſt the ſaile,
Yet Galleys may by the maine force of ore,
So much againſt the ſpite of winds preuaile,
To come with ſafety to the merry ſhore.
What if one meane or purpoſe hap to faile,
Is that a reaſon we ſhould trie no more?　(good:
　　This will not ſerue, what though? that may be
　Is there no way but one vnto the wood?

　　　　　　　　　　　　　　　When

EMBLEME XLIIII.

When warres and troubles most molest,
The wicked persons prosper best.

To fish for Eeles, they say that haue the skill,
Best be the troubled waters and the muddie:
So they that take delight in doing ill,
To trouble first the state is all their studie;
Then can they best compasse their wicked will,
And get most profit when the times be bloudy.
  Iustice in force, peaceable times and quiet
  Fits not their fishing, nor can serue their diet.

EMBLEME XLV.

Beware of fained flattering showes,
For none are worse then friendly foes.

False flatterers are worse then greedie crowes:
Crowes onely feed on things that we reiect,
The flatterers do oft deuowre those,
That are aliue, when least they do suspect.
And when they make their fairest glosing shoes,
And seeme most soundly friendship to affect,
  Then suddenly, and ere a man is ware,
  He is beguil'd and falleth in their snare.

The

EMBLEME XLVI.

The learned liue but poore and bare,
When fooles be rich and better fare.

Who giues an asse the bone, a dog the hay,
May well be thought an vnwise man I trow:
Yet such disorder waxeth now aday,
Men care not how their gifts they do bestow.
Fooles are set vp in offices most gay,
The wiser men come downe and sit below.
  And now affection reason so doth smother,
  Men giue to one what doth belong t'another.

EMBLEME XLVII.

The child procures his parents ruth,
That is not chastis'd in his youth.

The Ape embracing of her yong one hard,
Sometimes doth kill it with her being kind.
So many parents haue their children mard,
When with fond loue and with affection blind,
They cannot chastise them with due regard,
That in their childhood be not well inclin'd.
  For when they be growne vp to state of men,
  They are past mending and correcting then.

EMBLEME XLVIII.

Disguised things may seeme most strange,
But nature seeld is seene to change.

Bacchus cannot himselfe so well disguise,
By clapping on his backe a Lyons skin,
But that his flagon and his bolle descries,
It is no *Hercules* that is within.
So though a foole haue shew of being wise,
By hoarie head, or by a bearded chin:
   Yet by his talke a man may quickly know,
   Whether he be discreete indeed or no.

EMBLEME XLIX.

The rich men sinne and feare no lawes,
When poore are punisht for light cause.

The Spider with her web of rare inuention,
Lies close in waite to catch the silly flies;
But with the wasp she dares not moue contentiō,
Whose force the weakenesse of her web vnties.
So rich men now against all good intentiō, (lies,
Withstād good laws, whose weight on poore mē
  And like the wasp that rends the web in sunder,
  They rule those laws that meaner mē are vnder

Malicious

EMBLEME L.

Malicious fooles worke most disgrace,
When they are set in highest place.

Who giues him wine a feauer doth possesse,
Augmenteth more the patients present griefe:
Wine causeth heate, the feauer doth no lesse,
Which needs must yeeld the sick but smal reliefe.
Eu'n so that Prince doth little skill professe,
That sets a foole aloft in office chiefe,
   Whereas his malice he may best reueale,
   And do most hurt vnto the common weale.

EMBLEME LI.

After youth in trauell spent,
Let age be with her home content.

The painfull Pilgrime in his later daies:
Without his leaning staffe that cannot stand,
Forsaking wife and children goes his waies,
To seeke old relicks in a new found land;
Accounting it worth most especiall praise,
To tell what iourneyes he hath tane in hand:
  Whē he should cut those wings if he did well,
  And like the Tortesse keepe him in his shell.

With

EMBLEME LII.

With diligence we ought to wayt,
To flie the snares of false deceit.

The Eagle then laments her death too late,
When as the shaft hath pierced through her brest,
Who was selfe cause of such vnluckie fate,
By meanes the stem with her own quill was drest.
Some men to ill are so predestinate,
That though no hurt by others is profest,
    They wrong theselues by lack of taking heed,
    And are chiefe cause of their owne euill speed.

EMBLEME LIII.

The liues of Princes lewdly led,
About the world are soonest spred.

Each little spot appeares more in the face,
Than any blemish in the corps beside:
The face is plainly seene in euery place,
When clothes the carkasse secretly do hide.
By which we note, that in a Princes grace.
A fault seemes greater and is sooner spide,
    Than in some man of base and low degree:
    As in fine cloth the brightest staines we see.

The

EMBLEME LIIII.

The Prince that would beware of harme,
Must stop his eares: o flatterers charme.

When the wise birder meaneth to intrap
The foolish birds within his craftie traine,
That he may get more of them at a clap,
With prettie pipe his voice he learnes to faine.
So flatterers do not display the map
Of all their drifts in termes and speches plaine,
  But with sweet words they couer their deceit,
  Lest princes should perceiue & shun their bait.

E

EMBLEME LV.

Wit can do with little paine,
That strength alone cannot attaine.

A man by force and strength cannot attaine,
That which by staid discretion soone is wonne:
He that doth pull the taile with might and maine,
For all his force hath not so quickly done,
The other haire by haire with little paine,
In lesser time a better threed hath sponne.

   Lo here the ods betweene the wise mans pause,
And hastinesse of foolish furious dawes.

More

EMBLEME LVI.

More die with surfet at their boord,
Then in the warres with dint of sword.

The glut'nous Rau'n deuours the venomd Snake,
Which though at first seemes pleasant to his taste,
When he doth feele his gorge with poison ake,
He rues with death the meate he eat in haste.
Hereby we note what heed we ought to take,
Lest that we vse excesse in our repast:
  For gluttony doth more their deaths affoord,
  Then mightie *Mars* with his two edged sword.

EMBLEME LVII.

He that is prowd'st of good hap,
Sorrow fals soonest in his lap.

Iupiter, as the learned *Homer* writes,
Mingleth the good and bad in such a sort,
That men obtaine not pleasures and delights,
Without some paine to waite vpon the sport.
No man with labour wearieth so his sprights,
But of some ease withall he may report:
  Nor no man yet hath euer bene so glad,
  But he hath had a time to be as sad.

Vaine

EMBLEME LVIII

Vaine hope doth oft a man allure,
A needlesse bondage to endure.

Who so to bondage will himselfe submit,
And yet hath libertie to liue at will,
Is like a Lyon when he doth permit
A simple man with threed to hold him still.
Some are such fooles, that while in court they sit,
And waste their time and all their riches spill:
    Yet will they stay, although they do not need,
    And not escape whē they may break the threed.

EMBLEME LIX.

He that to thrift his mind would frame,
Must not delight to follow game.

It is no time to sit still then at play,
When as the house doth burne about our eares:
Who were in flames, and would not run away,
Were wondrous stout, or very void of feares.
But wisedome bids vs shorten long delay,
And to preuent the cause of future teares:
  Sith if too farre we suffer dangers rome,
  Tis long againe ere they be ouercome.

A

EMBLEME LX.

A man of courage and of spright,
No foolish threatning can affright.

Who thinks to feare the Lyon with a maske,
May proue conclusions, but preuaile no whit:
For why, his force a stouter strength doth aske,
Ere that his courage can be quaild with it.
So some we see do set their tongues to taske,
And with great words that run beyond their wit,
  They thinke to conquer hardie men and stout,
  That of vaine brags do neither dread nor doubt.

E 4

EMBLEME LXI.

The man whose conscience is vnpure,
In his owne mind he is not sure.

The wicked man whose faults are manifest,
Seemes like the Hare still full of feare and dread:
He dares not sleepe nor take his quiet rest,
For doubt before some Iustice to be led.
The honest life who leades is better blest:
He euermore secure may keepe his bed,
  The while the wicked studie and deuise,
  Like fearefull Hares to sleepe with open eyes.

Where

EMBLEME LXII.

*Where Cupid list to play the knaue,
He makes the Asse to brag and braue.*

When Cupids stroke tickles the inward vaines,
Oh what a power he hath to change the mind!
He makes the niggard carelesse of his gaines,
The clowne a Courtier, and the currish kind.
Briefly, his wondrous graces where he raignes,
In *Cymon* our of *Boccas* you may find;
   The little lad his Lute can finger so,
     Would make an Asse to turne vpon the toe.

EMBLEME LXIII.

It is a point of no small cunning,
To catch Occasion at her coming.

Behold Occasion drawne before your eies,
As though she still were fleeting on her waies,
Which image so *Lisippus* did deuise,
With knife in hand to cut off long delayes.
Her locks before bids hold ere that she flies,
Her wings do shew she can abide no staies:
   And by her bald she tels vs at the last,
   There is no hold behind when she is past.

The

EMBLEME LXIIII.

The praise of beauty is but small,
Where vertue is not ioynd withall.

By mens proportions we can hardly guesse,
Or know precisely whether they haue wit:
For who can tell what graces they possesse,
Although their members out of order sit?
Some heads are great, and some againe be lesse,
That to their bodies do not aptly fit:
   Yet not proportion nor the bodies stature,
   But education setteth foorth the nature.

EMBLEME LXV.

The fairest shape of th'outward part,
Shewes not the vertues of the heart.

The stately Cypresse in his outward show,
Is straight and tall, in colour fresh and greene;
Yet on the same no wholesome fruit doth grow,
Or that to serue for nourishment is seene.
In such bare titles many men do flow,
That in their liues but barren still haue bene:
  Who in experience well may seeme to sute
  The Cypres tree that yeelds no wholsom fruite.

Annoint

EMBLEME LXVI.

Annoint the Lawyer in his fist,
And he shall pleade eu'n what you list.

Some Lawyers waxe so deafe they cannot heare,
Or at the least they cannot vnderstand,
Except your money do so plaine appeare,
That palpably they feele it in their hand.
Giue right or wrong, your case they say is cleare;
As you would haue it, so it shall be scand.
    When double fees do walke, and money flees,
    A man would think their hands were ful of eies.

EMBLEME LXVII.

Let fire or sword their choler wreake,
A constant heart can nothing breake.

Like to the Stith I count the constant hart:
The Stith endures the heauie hammers beat,
And doth not shrinke nor yeeld in any part,
Though smiths lay on & thump it till they sweat.
Eu'n so should men in chances ouerthwart,
Whē paines increase & fortune seemes to threat,
  Yet in their course with constant purpose run,
  And still persist till they haue honour wonne.

When

EMBLEME LXVIII.

When youth is in his flowring prime,
He cares not how he passe his time.

Redeeme the time, time dearer is then gold,
And time once gone can neuer be reclaimed,
He need begin betimes that would grow old,
If time be lost, our life is likewise maimed.
Yet greene yong heads disdaining to be told,
As though more priuiledge of yeres they claimed,
   Do seem to pul the weights with all their sway,
   And waste their time, and haste their dying day.

EMBLEME LXIX.

He that himselfe is void of wit,
In a wise man despiseth it.

Some say, the Camell will not stoope to drinke,
Till he hath first defil'd it with his feete.
So in our time rude people vse to thinke,
That perfect eloquence is most vnmeete:
In whose dull heads this reason will not sinke,
That eloquence should proue a thing so sweete;
  Such is their folly, and their sense so blind,
  They count this gift but of the basest kind.

Greedie

EMBLEME LXX.

Greedie gaping after gaine,
Will make a man take any paine.

The hope for gaine, and thirst for worldly goods
Compels a man to venture rocks and seas:
Neither can waters deepe, nor raging floods,
Cause any kind of perils to displease:
Men scrape out goods out of the myrie muds,
For lucres sake, all labours seeme but ease:
  And to prouide themselues of things they lack,
  There be wil swim with burdens on their back.

EMBLEME LXXI.

There is no thing can be more deere,
Than Time, if we could keepe it heare.

The fleeting time doth quickly steale away,
Which once let passe, returneth not againe,
Therefore tis good to take Time while we may,
Lest afterward we rue our losse in vaine:
Time tarrieth none, the Prouerbe old doth say,
Then vse it well the while it doth remaine:
    For those that leade their liues in belly-cheare,
    Do leese their time, of al things else most deare.

In

EMBLEME LXXII.

In time all things shall be reuealed,
That are most secretly concealed.

Greene fruits and floures do ripen by the Sunne,
Whose raies bring forth their beautie and their smel:
Eu'n so when youth with time is ouer-run,
Though it were greene, and though it often fell,
Yet riper yeares will mend all errors done,
And make men liue more vertuously, and well:
  And time doth change and alter mens behauior,
  As by the Sunne the flowers mend their sauor.

EMBLEME LXXIII.

A traitor and a flattering friend,
Say that they neuer do intend.

The flatterers and traitors both be such,
That with their words their thoughts do not a-
For till iust triall bring them to the tuch, (gree:
They seeme in shew most faithfull friends to bee:
But little will they do, professing much;
And inwardly from friendship they do flee;
  Who when their heart behind they do conuay,
  They beare in hand their tongue another way.

With

EMBLEME LXXIIII.

With some light thing when thou needs must,
Trie thou thy friend before thou trust.

We proue at first if that a pot will hold,
With water, not with wine of any kind,
To th'end the losse the lesse we may behold,
If in the bottome any hole we find.
So ere to trust a stranger ye waxe bold,
Tell him the lightest secret of your mind,
    Whereof small danger growes another day,
    If he againe your secret should bewray.

EMBLEME LXXV.

Reason bids vs haue a care,
That others harmes make vs beware.

In Affrica if Lions hanged there,
Do terrifie the rest that them behold,
Why do not theeues and robbers likewise feare,
That still commit most wicked acts for gold?
And Magistrates that such great office beare,
By like examples feare to be too bold:
   For they may know, except they do amend,
   By such lewd liuing they may haue like end.

We

EMBLEME LXXVI.

We purchase nothing by our play,
But beggery and our decay.

They that do vse to hazard much at play,
And venture all their substance at a cast,
Do often fall into so great decay,
That they become meere beggers at the last:
And then on others they are faine to pray,
Or liue of spoile, and others goods to wast:
 When as their owne before with better thrift,
 Would well haue seru'd their turn at eu'ry shift.

EMBLEME LXXVII.

All those that loue do fancie must,
But lose their labour and their cost.

Fond loue is chiefly likened to a siue,
In which the more you poure the water in,
The more is spilt, by letting thorow driue,
And you no neare then when you first begin.
Eu'n so for loue when yong men frankly giue,
Till oft they leaue themselues not worth a pin:
   When all is spent, and they liue by the losse,
   They turne againe at last by weeping crosse.

EMBLEME LXXVIII.

A woman is of such a kind,
That nothing can content her mind.

Who so a ship would vndertake to store,
And furnish her with all that she doth lacke:
He needs to haue his purse well lin'd before,
And shall find worke enough to hold him tacke.
Yet women are as chargeable, or more,
Who still are wanting one or other knacke:
  So that who would be troubled all his life,
  May best be troubled with a ship or wife.

EMBLEME LXXIX.

*A thousand dangers dayly grow,
Of foolish Loue, as louers know.*

Alas that men should follow Venus trace,
And take delight to play on Cupids bits,
Who casteth downe from high estate to base,
And makes men counted wise, to leese their wits.
None but vnhappy wretches void of grace,
Do euer fall into such franticke fits:
   Vpon repentance fire he puts the Still   (distill.
   And blowes the coles, where nought but teares
The

EMBLEME LXXX.

The fruite of loue is very strange,
It hath so many kinds of change.

The fruits of Loue are diuers in effect, (greene,
Some good, some bad, some withered, some are,
Some sweet, some soure, som wholsom, som infect,
And some are secret, some are plainely seene:
Now in regard; to morrow quite reiect;
Oft in prosperitie; and then in teene:
   They change as often, and do alter soone,
   Eu'n as vnconstant as we see the Moone.

EMBLEME LXXXI.

In all his stockes blind Loue doth set
The graffes of griefe, our hearts to fret.

If any man a perfect Gardiner lacks,
Here shall he find one of no common skill,
For sundry graffes, for knots and prettie knacks,
He neuer will be idle by his will.
What euer he doth set or sow, will waxe,
And all your stocks with some plants he will fill:
  But with the rest he graffeth alwaies chiefe,
  The choaking peare of anguish and of griefe.
                    Ungrate-

EMBLEME LXXXII.

Vngratefull men breed great offence,
As persons void of wit or sence.

The Oke doth suffer the yong Iuie wind
Vp by his sides, till it be got on hie:
But being got aloft, it so doth bind,
It kils the stocke that it was raised by.
So some proue so vnthankfull and vnkind
To those on whom they chiefly do rely,
    By whom they first were called to their state,
    They be the first (I say) giue them the mate.

EMBLEME LXXXIII.

It is a point of great foresight,
Into our selues to looke aright.

We reade how in Phœnicia long ago,
The people raisd this figure vp on hie,
Whereas the same might make the fairest show,
And men obserue what it did signifie.
The Serpent in a circle painted so,
Thus much doth teach to vnderstand thereby,
  That in the world there is no greater art,
  Then man to know himselfe in euery part.

On

EMBLEME LXXXIIII.

On others some presume to pray,
And fall themselues into decay.

The Faulcon sometime greedie of her pray,
Finds her owne foote fast tide vnto the tree:
So are there some lay waite on others way,
That are themselues the first that harmed bee.
Who digs a pit for other mens decay,
May fall therein himselfe we often see,
    And feele the plagues in his own person then,
    Which he ordaind to punish other men.

EMBLEME LXXXV.

Who labours that to bring to passe,
That cannot be, is but an asse.

The cannon charg'd with lesse then doth behoue,
The heauie bullet farre off cannot throw:
And none hath seene the weighty windmil moue
If one but with a paire of bellowes blow.
This shewes we should in euery action proue
With due proportion how each thing should go:
  As wise men neuer will attempt the thing,
  That first they know to passe they cannot bring.

EMBLEME LXXXVI.

The Prelates life should shine as cleare,
As lampe on mountaine doth appeare.

The Prelates vertues ought to shine so bright,
As doth a lampe set on a mountaine hie,
From whose good deeds should issue such a light
That other men might see and walke thereby.
Through his example when it is not right,
The silly people oft do walke awry; (stands
  And then the Lord whose vengeance none with-
  The bloud of those requireth at his hands.

G

EMBLEME LXXXVII.

In euery thing aduise you first:
Take the best, and leaue the worst.

In Poets pamphlets fables fond we find,
Yet in those fables wisedome they inuent;
The morall still hath sense of other kind,
How ere the verse do colour their intent:
But to the letter who himselfe doth bind,
May misse the matter that therein is meant:
  As vnder leaues that hang on crooked vines,
  Lie hid sweet grapes that make the costly wines.

No

EMBLEME LXXXVIII.

No surety in a womans minde,
Her fancie changeth with the winde.

A womans constancy is euen as sure,
As if one held an Eele fast by the taile,
Her faith nor loue do neuer long endure,
But fleete away as Sunne doth melt the haile:
As many authors, Greeke and Latine pure,
Haue left in writing for our more auaile,
   That womens words mens eares do so delight,
   They make them oft beleeue the crow is white.

EMBLEME LXXXIX.

No shade of enuy can obscure,
The light of vertue shining pure.

When as the Sunne stands iust aboue the head,
The bodie shewes but short and slender shade;
Eu'n so whē vertue her bright beames doth spred
The smoke of enuy soone away doth fade.
Vertue doth make men liue when they be dead,
Though enuy brag, & thogh she draw her blade,
  In spite thereof yet vertuous men shall gaine
    Honour and praise, for euer to remaine.

A

EMBLEME XC.

A worde once spoken though in vaine,
It cannot be recald againe.

It is too late to catch the bird againe,
That once hath bid her keepers hand adue:
So when a man lets slip a word in vaine,
His speech once past is not recald anew;
For words will flie from mouth to mouth amaine
Whereof great quarrels oftentimes ensue.
  Therefore be wise, and in your speech preuent,
  To speak such words as you may chance repent.

EMBLEME XCI.

*None waxe more proud we lightly see,
Then beggers rais'd to high degree.*

Bucephalus was then in chiefest pride,
When he had felt rich armour on his backe,
And onely *Alexander* him might ride,
When no man else could hold him any tacke.
Hereby we note a ahing that oft is tride,
How such as are but base and in great lacke,
   When to new honor by good hap they grow,
   Their old acquaintance they disdaine to know.

Loue

EMBLEME XC.

Loue and feare are chiefest things,
That stablish Scepters vnto kings.

A Prince that would his fame should stil increase,
And honour to resound in euery place,
He shall assure his Scepter with more ease,
If that his subiects loue and feare his face.
A Dog and Hare two enemies to peace,
One loues, the other feareth in like case:
  Yet better peace to Princes neuer springs,
  Then when like Dogs and Hares men serue their
                                    (kings.

EMBLEME XCIII.

He that would loade a happie life,
For vertue let him chuse his wife.

Some do not care how nor with whó they linke,
If fading beauty please their wanton eye:
Others so they be fingring of the chinke,
Care not how soone their hand be in the pie;
But a wise man doth warily forethinke,
That both those courses run too farre awrie:
   That this nor that, is neither here nor there,
   The chiefest choice is chusing by the eare.

EMBLEME XCIIII.

No kind of friend will longer stay,
When riches once are gone away.

The lyce do shun the place where they were bred
When life to leaue the carkasse they do find:
So when mens fortune failes and waxeth dead,
And when their wealth and riches do vnwind,
We see the flatterers away are fled,
From those to whom the same were earst inclind.
   This shewes that in aduersity and need,
   Tis hard to finde a trustie friend indeed.

EMBLEME XCV.

When thou for ayd to God doſt pray,
To helpe thy ſelfe thou muſt aſſay.

When thou ſhalt trauell on the tedious way,
And ſee thy Aſſe fall loden in the mire,
Firſt for the helpe of God prepare to pray,
That ſuccours all that do his helpe require;
But in the meane time ceaſſe not to aſſay,
With thy owne hands to draw him from the mire.
   For he that would the helpe of God attaine,
   To helpe himſelfe muſt take a little paine.

EMBLEME XCVI.

A wanton woman and a light,
Will not be tam'd by art nor might.

With greater ease the Dolphin is restrained,
Then wanton women bridled of their will,
Who from their purpose cannot be constrained.
They are so full of craft and subtill skill:
Wel may they boast what guerdõ they haue gai- (ned,
That can subiect their wiues vnto their will;
  For oft the ayer of a womans smocke,
    Withstands alone the bonds of chast wedlock.

EMBLEME XCVII.

Constancie hath most renowne,
When crosses most do beate vs downe.

The more that Saffron troden is with feete,
The more it still doth flourish on the ground:
So when with troubles vertuous minds do meet,
The more opprest, the stronger they be found.
Where vertue is, there may we plainest see't,
In those whom cares & woes do compasse round:
   And when aduersity doth most assaile,
  By striuing then aloft to beare their saile.

Who

EMBLEME XCVIII.

Who so to studie doth incline,
The hardest wit it shall refine.

Though childrens wit be not so ripe and quicke,
As vnto others nature doth impart,
Paine wil helpe out where nature seemes to stick,
And they great maisters made of many an art;
Eu'n as the Beare doth into fashion licke,
The lump she laid without proportiond part;
   For man is made againe by reasons helpe,
   As is new moulded the miss-shapen whelpe.

EMBLEME XCIX.

When some thinke most themselues in peace,
Their dangers oft do most increase.

When *Hercles* had ordaind to take his rest,
And from his former labours him withdrew,
Hydra that monstrous seuen-headed beast
Against him came, his troubles to renew.
Euen so when vertue hath her hire possest,
And once attained vnto honour due,
  Some chance or other by fowle enuy growes,
  And still new troubles and new trauels sowes.

The

EMBLEME C.

The hand that idlenesse detests,
Doth hoord the money in the chests.

Behold how Diligence as she were wroth,
Sits in her charriot with a scourge in hand,
And whippeth Idlenesse now for her sloth,
That of her need before time had not scand:
The little Ants take paines and draw them both,
Which giues vs this thereby to vnderstand,
  That lest we labour with the little Ant,
  We still are like to liue in wo and want.